*Traditional Recipes with a Flair*



Junior League of Binghamton, Inc.
Binghamton, New York

We proudly dedicate this collection of recipes from members and friends of the Junior League of Binghamton to League volunteers, past and present, in celebration of the Sixtieth Anniversary of our founding. We do not claim that all of our recipes are original, but they are our favorites and have been tested and retested and are ready to share with *your*

Cover and artwork generously underwritten by Giant Food Markets



| First printing | April 1992 | 10,000 copies |
| --- | --- | --- |
| Second printing | August 1993 | 10,000 copies |



ISBN 0-9607714-1-7

Library of Congress Card Catalog: 91-077886

Printed in the USA by

# TABLE OF CONTENTS



*Page*

# *About The Cover*

As a medium, paper sculpture is a method of making images that, even on the printed page, appear to have a three-dimensional quality. A gifted and skillful artist can create stunningly complicated designs despite the fact that there are only four things you can do to paper: you can cut it, bend it, fold it, or condition the surface. After creativity, craftsmanship is the most important aspect of paper sculpture.

Leo Monahan has established himself as one of the pre-eminent paper sculptors in the United States. His work has been exhibited in the Smithsonian Institution and the Pentagon and is included in numerous private collections. In addition, he was recently awarded the Los Angeles Society of Illustrators Life Achievement Award for his thirty years of illustration excellence. Mr. Monahan currently resides in Los Angeles, California.

We are proud to display the original cover artwork in the offices of the Junior League of Binghamton, thanks to a generous donation by Giant Food Markets.

# *The Cookbook Committee*

*Chair* .......... Kate M. Stacy
*Production Chair* .......... Nancy Sherwood
*Marketing Chair* .......... Sandy Griffiths
*Editor* .......... Liz Anderson
*Co-Editor & Recipe Chair* .......... Diana Auchter
*Recipe Chair* .......... Kathy Robilotto
*Design & Layout* .......... Nancy Shuman
*Secretary* .......... Debbie Kamlet
*Treasurer* .......... Mary S. Foley
*Distribution* .......... Mary E. Murphy
*Public Relations* .......... Nancy Hargrave
*Sustainer Representation* .......... Jane McGovern
Alice Schwartz

*Special thanks to our President, Joan Lacey, and to our Office Secretary, Rose Teegarden, for their endless hours of typing, typing, and re-typing...*

# *About Our League*

Since 1932 the members of the Junior League of Binghamton, Inc. have been improving the quality of life in the Southern Tier of New York State through their volunteer efforts. They have provided the personal time and financial aid to implement programs concerning the elderly, child advocacy, historical preservation, substance abuse, domestic violence, public education, and the arts.

The proceeds from the sale of *Family & Company* will be returned to the community through the League's support of these and other volunteer projects in a continuing effort to meet the changing needs of our community.

The Junior League of Binghamton, Inc. is an organization of women committed to promoting voluntarism and to improving the community through the effective action and leadership of trained volunteers. Its purposes are exclusively educational and charitable.

The League reaches out to all women 21 to 45 years of age, regardless of race, color, religion, or national origin, who demonstrate an interest in and commitment to voluntarism.

# About Our Community

The city of Binghamton is conveniently nestled at the confluence of the Susquehanna and Chenango Rivers. The Iroquois paddled their waters and maintained villages on their shores. Merchants and farmers found their banks rich with natural resources. Lumber was rafted and goods transported along the river currents as far as the Chesapeake Bay. The Chenango Canal connected Binghamton to the upstate regions of New York and served to transport eager, new families into the valley. The two rivers brought promise of prosperity and the good life.

Binghamton basks in the aura of families — their histories, traditions, and cultures. The community was inspired by a corps of families collaborating to determine the pace, pulse, and prosperity of a recognizably unique village. Family names — Bingham, Whitney, Hooper, Dickinson, Clark, Kilmer, Ross, Ford, Johnson, Watson, and Link — resound throughout the region as the perpetuators of our economy and growth. Cigars, shoes, time clocks, computers, aircraft, false teeth, and Swamp Root form a patent collage of commodities that made an impact on our entire nation.

Between 1890 and 1920 new directions and opportunities beckoned immigrants from Great Britain, Italy, Greece, and Eastern Europe. A "Valley of Opportunity" welcomed these families who would bring new life and a new culture to a community in progress. Today, the third generation of these immigrant families sustains the vibrancy and heartbeat of our existence. The diversity of cultures continues to make our communities shimmer with life.

We are a self-sustaining and stimulating community. Two institutions of higher learning grace the banks of our rivers. We trust a regional museum and a historical society to preserve our history, and we offer a hands-on museum to inspire our children. An impressive roster of visual artists, craftpersons, and performing arts organizations, keep the art spirit alive and well in all of us.

This is a community that glows with character and bursts with pride. We have accepted people—all people; we have accepted our geography and our weather; we have accepted corporate giants and the family-run corner store. We have learned to live with change, yet we will always share nostalgic memories of "Which way EJ?", the Phoebe Snow, the Pavilion, Ty Cobb, Slam Stewart, Rod Serling, floods, bridges, trolley cars, and carousels.

Thus, we offer, with great pleasure, our traditional recipes, happily bound in a cookbook that is meant for anyone who enjoys both good food and hospitality, and who wants to create them with style and ease! Whether we are serving Spiedies to family or Lobster Stuffed Tenderloin to company, our culinary style connects us to a very special heritage. So, prepare the festive board, assemble the family, welcome the company, and together, enjoy every morsel.

In the year '27, a prominent few
decided to find something worthwhile to do.
After days of much planning, long meetings, fatigue
they presented with pride… *The Binghamton Charity League.*

Its purpose, which continues, was fostering causes,
and its good works were met with acclaim and applauses.
The year '32 saw a memorable day
when the Charity League was accepted by AJLI.

And then did those ladies get on with a show
to lay the foundation for the League we now know.
They ignited more projects and fanned more good deeds
to help our fair city meet some of its needs.

The *Thrift Shop* appeared — that famous old store —
it was manned by the "flappers" and had clients galore!
A community trust fund, *The Day Nursery*, too
furnishing homes for the aged — those projects just flew.

They gave teas, they held dances, their roadsters were zooming
and by giving their all the trust fund was booming!
Yet, times were a-changing, the town really grew,
a new era would bring more changes to view.

The League did not panic, it assessed this new drift,
and with plotting and planning, the transition was swift.
Meet critical needs, address issues that count
human kind is the target; there are bad times to surmount.

*Continued on next page*

On the serious side, their hard work was done,
 but they balanced that service with projects for fun.
Remember the glee club — those rare vocal jewels?
 and the famous handpuppets — the delight of the schools.

They closed out the *Thrift Shop*, but picked up a star
 by presenting the annual *Bargain Bazaar.*
A big vote for kids, a new phase to enter
 with a hands-on for children, née *Discovery Center.*

*Safety Town* gives kids confidence to and from schools
 how to cross at intersections, how to follow the rules.
They opened a station for lives helter skelter
 a short-term abuse center, called *The Children's Shelter.*

A communication line for adult and child voices
 a serious talk with mom alone is appropriately called *Choices.*
For the '90's, local issues will each have a turn;
 housing homeless, helping children are both our concern.

The deeds go on forever; we cannot list them all,
 but, we're proud to say in sixty years we've tried to answer every call.
We've been through a depression, three long years and more
 yet we've overcome obstacles and we're always here for more!
So a great *Hurrah* for sixty years! We celebrate with pride
 and hope that strength and courage may continue as our guide.

— *Pokey Crocker*

# CELEBRITY CONTRIBUTIONS



*A sincere thank you to our celebrities, some local, some national, who have kindly permitted us to include their recipes. We are grateful to them for allowing us to become members of their extended family.*

# *Kids' Favorites*

In *your* home there may be a shining star eager to help in preparing for the arrival of company. More than a delicious meal can result from time spent in the kitchen. Accept the offer of assistance from willing young hands, and you may discover that you've also created a happy memory. Here is a list of recipes that will allow your children's culinary talents to shine. They are sure to enjoy the act of filling, dipping, stacking, frosting, pouring, and assembling. Everyone will bask in the glow of their accomplishments. So, enjoy (and eat) their concoctions!

*Page*

## *The Family Dinner*

*Sunday dinner...the family gathers...memories are shared...*

Welcome to Binghamton, New York, where traditional neighborhoods still exist, where grandparents pick up grandchildren from the same school they once attended, and children are treated to cookies made from a recipe passed down for generations. Step back from today's hectic pace, settle in, and rekindle family ties with our Family Dinner.

Leek and Asparagus Bisque

Orange Pork Tenderloin
Green Beans with Warm Mustard Vinaigrette
Cinnamon Spiced Rice

Sour Cream Poundcake with Strawberries Romanov

Pinot Noir

## *Company's Coming*

*China...linen...fresh flowers...*

What better way to pass a chilly January night in upstate New York than to invite close friends to share an evening at your home. Arrange the flowers, light the candles, select the music, and create an atmosphere of subtle elegance.

Asparagus with Honey Mustard Dip
Crab Won Tons

Sherried Brie Soup
Chilled Fino Sherry

Lobster Stuffed Tenderloin of Beef
Spinach Soufflé Filled Tomato Cups
Potato, Shitake, and Brie Gratin
Aged French Bordeaux

Gateau au Chocolat
Ruby Port

## *The Brunch*

*Autumn harvest...falling leaves...friends both old and new...*

Early October in upstate New York is breathtaking and offers an excellent opportunity to invite out-of-town guests to witness the foliage at its peak. Begin the day with a walk in the woods, gather friends and neighbors to partake in this delicious brunch, and spend the afternoon cheering for your favorite team.

24-Hour Omelette
Puffed Pancake with Strawberries
Gingerbread Waffles
Assorted Fresh Fruits
Pumpkin Apple Streusel Muffins
Sour Cream Coffee Cake
Orange Blush Crêpes

Indian Summer Punch

## *The Luncheon*

*Lace tablecloths...an heirloom punch bowl...the guest of honor...*

The mood has been set for an engagement party, bridal luncheon, or baby shower. Family and company arrive, eager to spend time together, to share in celebrating one of life's memorable occasions, and to indulge in this sumptuous buffet.

Chilled Cucumber Soup

Crustless Crab Quiche
Lemon Ginger Chicken Salad
Mixed Salad Greens with Homemade French Dressing
Toasted Coconut Bread

Butterfly Cookies
Chocolate Mousse Torte

Kir with Ice Garland

## *The Birthday Party*

*The anticipation...the arrival...the festivities begin...*

Next to the holidays, a child's birthday is the highlight of the year. Every mother wants the celebration to be a success. Broome County is home to six historic carousels, and an outing to any one of them is sure to make your birthday affair a memorable one. Upon your return home, satisfy appetites with homemade pretzels, ice cream cones, and sugarplum cake.

Lollipops and Soft Pretzels

Tempting Chicken Tenders
Strawberry Pretzel Salad
Kid's Crudités (Carrot Curls and Celery Boats)

Sugarplum Cake with Gumdrop Garnish
Ice Cream Cones

Creamiscle Punch

## *The Casual Get-Together*

*Saturday night...after the game...the gang's all here...*

Roll up the rug, get out the CD's, set up the Ping-Pong table, and the teenagers' party is underway. Your teen can be in charge of preparing the food from the Pizza Salad to the Kids' Colada. They will be proud to serve this to their friends and may even help with the clean up!

Pizza Salad
Chips and Fresh Dill Dip

Sloppy Beef
Hot Dogs with Sauce
Oven Baked Potato Wedges
Tortellini-Broccoli Salad

Giant Killer Cake
Snickerdoodles

Kids' Colada

## *The Dinner for Two*

*Champagne... candlelight... a private celebration...*

Upstate New Yorkers are privileged to have many small lakes nestled in their countryside. A quiet weekend at a lakeside cottage provides the perfect setting for a romantic dinner for two. Having spent a little extra time preparing the meal, you can now relax, look out across the water, and cherish these tender moments.

Spaghetti with Mushroom Champagne Sauce
Champagne or Sparkling Wine

Orange and Romaine Toss
Sole and Salmon Pinwheels
Carrots and Green Grapes
Heirloom Wheat Crescents
Treleaven Reserve Chardonnay (New York State)

Soufflé au Grand Marnier
New York State Ice Wine

## *The Cocktail Party*

*Easy conversation... good cheer... a relaxed hostess...*

Line your walk with potted flowers, hang a new wreath to reflect the season, and greet your guests with a frozen margarita. Offer a bountiful basket of crudités alongside an assortment of hearty appetizers, and your guests — from the first to arrive to the last to leave — are sure to find the samplings irresistible.

Sassy Southern Tier Shrimp
Coconut Chicken with Duck Sauce
Mini Hamburgers
New Potatoes with Sour Cream and Bacon
Herb and Mushroom Puff Pastries
Cheese Ramekin
Crudités with Water Chestnut Dip
Frozen Margaritas
A selection of wines including Pinot Grigio and White Zinfandel

## *The Family Reunion*

*Family arrives...news is shared...food is prepared...*

Many residents of the Binghamton area have grandparents who passed through Ellis Island on their way to the Southern Tier. The Family Reunion was born of an eagerness to establish Old World traditions in a new home, a new culture, a new country. At such an event, traditions, secret recipes, and tales of family exploits are passed on. Sample this fare as you celebrate the gathering of your family.

Fresh Fruit with Kahlúa Dip
Pecan Fried Chicken
London Broil with Fabulous Teriyaki Marinade
Tomato and Mozzarella with Fresh Basil
Classic Coleslaw
Wild Rice Salad
Stuffed Zucchini

Apple Crisp Pie
Magnificent Mocha Pie
Mom's Frozen Lemon Pie

## *The Company Picnic*

*Work's left behind...everyone relaxes...the fun begins...*

Whether they work for IBM, Endicott Johnson, or one of the smaller corporations, when Southern Tier employees head off to the company picnic, they often go to one of our stunning State parks. With children in tow, all arrive eager for the softball game or three-legged races to begin. Red and white tablecloths dot the pavilions as the aroma of grilled spiedies fills the air. As the party winds down, everyone leaves satisfied and with a renewed sense of camaraderie.

Vegetable Pizza
Honest-to-Goodness Barbecue Wings
Crunchy Broccoli Salad
Country Inn Potato Salad
Grilled Chicken Marinade
"The Original" Lamb Spiedies
Ratatouille
Wild Rice Casserole

Carrot Cake with Cream Cheese Frosting
Black Bottom Cupcakes
World's Best Cookies

OPENERS
&
QUENCHERS

# OPENERS & QUENCHERS



*Appetizers*



*Dips*



*Beverages*

## *Sassy Southern Tier Shrimp*

*Begin with our best, as we did, for your family and company.*

- *1/2 cup olive or vegetable oil*
- *1/4 cup grapefruit juice*
- *1/4 cup tequila*
- *2 cloves garlic, minced*
- *1 teaspoon cumin*
- *1/2 teaspoon salt*
- *1/2 teaspoon sugar*
- *1/2 teaspoon bottled hot pepper sauce*
- *1 pound shrimp, peeled and deveined*

### *Avocado Sauce*

- *2 small ripe avocados, peeled and mashed*
- *1 small tomato, chopped*
- *1/4 cup chopped green chilies, drained*
- *1/4 cup minced onion*
- *1/4 cup sour cream*
- *2 tablespoons chopped cilantro*
- *1 tablespoon tequila*
- *1/2 teaspoon salt*

*Makes 16 to 20*

• *The Shrimp* — In a large bowl, combine oil, grapefruit juice, tequila, garlic, cumin, salt, sugar, and hot pepper sauce until well blended. Add shrimp; toss to coat well. Cover; refrigerate at least 2 hours, turning occasionally. Broil or grill 4 inches from source of heat for 4 to 5 minutes, turning once and brushing frequently with marinade. Serve with Avocado Sauce as a dip.

• *The Sauce* — In a small bowl, combine all ingredients until well blended. Cover; refrigerate.

# *Melon and Shrimp Kabobs*

*It's hard to imagine a more appealing kabob.*

- *3 cups cubed melon (cantaloupe, honeydew, or crenshaw)*
- *1 pound cooked shrimp, peeled and deveined (approximately 24 pieces)*
- *8 scallions, cut into 2-inch lengths*
- *1/4 cup sour cream*
- *1/4 cup lemon yogurt*
- *1 1/2 ounces cream cheese*
- *1 tablespoon lemon juice*
- *2 teaspoons curry powder*
- *1/4 cup shredded coconut*
- *1/4 teaspoon salt*
- *4-inch wooden skewers*

*Makes 12 to 16*

- In a blender or food processor, combine sour cream, yogurt, cream cheese, lemon juice, curry powder, coconut, and salt. Process until smooth. Cover and chill 3 to 4 hours.
- Skewer melon and shrimp on kabobs, alternating fruit and seafood. To add color, include a scallion, pierced crosswise, in center of kabob.
- Arrange kabobs on a platter. Serve curried yogurt coconut dressing alongside, to be used as dip.

# *Crispy Fried Shrimp*

*A crunchy version of your favorite shrimp tempura*

- *1 pound raw shrimp, peeled and deveined, tails intact*
- *1 egg, lightly beaten*
- *4 tablespoons cornstarch, divided*
- *1 teaspoon dry white wine*
- *½ teaspoon soy sauce*
- *¾ teaspoon salt, divided*
- *½ cup flour*
- *½ cup water*
- *1 tablespoon vegetable oil*
- *½ teaspoon baking soda*
- *vegetable oil for frying*
- *duck sauce*

*Makes 20 to 24*

- Slit shrimp lengthwise down the back, almost in half. Mix egg, 1 tablespoon cornstarch, wine, soy sauce, and ¼ teaspoon salt in a glass bowl; stir in shrimp. Cover and refrigerate 10 minutes.

- Mix flour, water, 3 tablespoons cornstarch, 1 tablespoon oil, baking soda, and ½ teaspoon salt. Stir shrimp into batter until coated. Fry 5 or 6 at a time in hot oil in a 3-quart saucepan, turning occasionally, until golden brown, 2 to 3 minutes; drain. Serve hot with duck sauce.

*Can be prepared several hours ahead and reheated in a 350° oven.*

## *Broiled Deviled Clams*

*A round of applause to Carol Burnett for sharing this with us*

- *24 small hard-shelled clams*
- *3/4 cup butter, softened*
- *3 tablespoons Dijon mustard*
- *1/4 cup minced shallots*
- *2 tablespoons lemon juice*
- *salt and pepper to taste*
- *stale bread crumbs*
- *rock salt*

*Makes 24*

- Clean and shuck clams. Discard top shell and release from bottom shell.
- In a bowl, combine butter, mustard, shallots, lemon juice, salt, and pepper. Divide butter mixture among the clams, spreading it evenly so that each clam is completely covered. Cover clams with plastic wrap and chill 30 minutes.
- Sprinkle 2 teaspoons of bread crumbs over each clam. Arrange on a bed of rock salt in a shallow baking pan. Broil clams 2 inches from heat source for 3 to 4 minutes, or until crumbs are golden.

## *Cheese Straws*

*Just perfect for unexpected company*

- *1 pound sharp cheese, grated*
- *1 3/4 cups flour*
- *1/2 cup butter, creamed*
- *1/2 teaspoon salt*
- *1/4 teaspoon cayenne pepper*
- *1/2 cup water*

- Mix together all ingredients. Roll out into a thin sheet. Cut into narrow strips, 4-inches long. Bake at 350° for 25 minutes, or until lightly browned.

*Straws can be frozen before baking.*

# *Mushrooms Stuffed with Clams*

*Stuffed mushrooms with a continental flair*

- 8-12 *ounces large, fresh mushrooms, caps left whole, stems removed and finely chopped*
- 1/4 *cup minced shallots*
- 3 *tablespoons butter, divided*
- 1 *large clove garlic, minced*
- 1 *slice white bread, coarsely crumbled*
- 1 *(6 1/2 ounce) can minced clams, drained*
- 2 *tablespoons finely chopped fresh parsley*
- 3 *tablespoons white wine*
- 1/4 *teaspoon tarragon*
- 1 *egg yolk*
- 3 *tablespoons heavy cream*
- *salt and pepper to taste*
- 3 *tablespoons grated Parmesan cheese*

*Makes 20 to 24*

- Sauté chopped mushroom stems with shallots in 1½ tablespoons butter until shallots are tender, adding garlic halfway through. Add bread, clams, 1 tablespoon parsley, wine, and tarragon.
- Beat egg yolk with cream. Remove clam mixture from heat. Add egg and cream mixture. Return to heat and cook 1 minute. Season to taste.
- Melt remaining butter and brush mushroom caps. Turn caps hollow-side up and fill with stuffing, mounding in center. Sprinkle with Parmesan cheese.
- Bake at 350° for 10 to 15 minutes, or until heated through. Sprinkle with remaining parsley.

## *Coconut Chicken*

*One of the true gems in our cookbook*

- *4-5 whole boneless, skinless, chicken breasts*
- *3 eggs*
- *1 (7 ounce) package shredded coconut*
- *¾ cup flour*
- *½ cup milk*
- *vegetable oil*
- *duck sauce*

*Makes 80 to 100*

- Cut chicken into bite-size pieces. Combine eggs, coconut, flour, and milk to make batter. Dredge chicken in batter to coat.
- Fry chicken pieces in oil until golden brown, turning often. Serve with duck sauce.

*Appetizers can be made ahead and frozen. When ready to serve, reheat at 350° for 10 minutes.*

## *Sesame Chicken Nuggets with Peanut Sauce*

*A change of pace*

- *1 tablespoon smooth peanut butter*
- *1 tablespoon soy sauce*
- *1 tablespoon rice vinegar or distilled white vinegar*
- *¼ teaspoon sesame oil*
- *¼ teaspoon dry red pepper flakes*
- *2 whole boneless, skinless chicken breasts, cut into 1½-inch pieces*
- *1 tablespoon toasted sesame seeds*
- *vegetable oil*

*Makes 30 to 40*

- To make dipping sauce, combine peanut butter, soy sauce, vinegar, sesame oil, and pepper flakes in a small bowl, stirring to blend. Set aside.
- Stir-fry chicken 4 to 6 minutes, or until browned. Remove from pan; toss with sesame seeds to coat. Serve with dipping sauce.

## *Rippled Beef*

*Handy and hearty*

*2 pounds flank steak*
*¾ teaspoon salt*
*½ teaspoon basil*
*⅛ teaspoon pepper*
*3 tablespoons sugar*
*½ cup orange juice*
*2 tablespoons vinegar*
*2 teaspoons lemon juice*
*1 teaspoon lime juice*
*1 teaspoon dry mustard*
*vegetable oil*
*6-inch wooden skewers*
*mushroom caps, green pepper, and onion wedges for garnish*

*Makes 24 to 30*

- Combine salt, basil, and pepper; rub mixture into meat. Slice meat across the grain into long, thin strips, approximately 1½-inches wide.

- Cook and stir sugar over low heat until caramel colored. Gradually add orange juice and vinegar, stirring until sugar dissolves. Cool. Stir in lemon and lime juices and mustard. Pour over beef. Cover and marinate overnight in refrigerator.

- Drain meat. Stir-fry slices in hot oil.

- Fold each strip of meat accordion-style. Pierce all layers of folded meat with a wooden skewer so meat forms a rippled pattern when folds are allowed to "relax."

- Garnish each skewer with a mushroom cap, cooked onion wedge, or piece of green pepper.

*Instead of stir-frying beef, place it on skewers before cooking. Grill beef 3 to 4 minutes.*

## *Honest-to-Goodness Barbecue Wings*

*Addictive!*

*½ cup vegetable oil*
*1 small onion, chopped*
*½ cup red wine vinegar*
*1 tablespoon Worcestershire sauce*
*½ cup lemon juice*
*¼ cup firmly packed brown sugar*
*2 cups ketchup*
*1 tablespoon paprika*
*salt and pepper to taste*
*40 chicken wings, split*

*Makes 40*

- Sauté onion in vegetable oil.
- Add remaining ingredients (except chicken wings) to onions and simmer 20 minutes. Cool marinade completely.
- Marinate wings in refrigerator at least 24 hours.
- Grill wings 20 minutes, basting frequently.

## *Mini Hamburgers*

*A welcome change from Swedish meatballs*

*¾ pound lean ground beef*
*1 teaspoon minced parsley*
*salt and pepper to taste*
*sliced bread*
*tomatoes, thinly sliced*
*onions, sliced into thin rings*

*Makes 18 to 20*

- Mix ground beef with parsley, salt, and pepper. Shape into tiny hamburgers, 1½ inches in diameter. Broil or grill 3 minutes per side.
- Cut bread into 1½-inch rounds. Bake on a cookie sheet at 350° until crispy and dry.
- Place hamburgers on toasted bread. Garnish with tomato and onion.

# *Two-Bite Tacos*

*Let the kids build their own and they'll come in droves.*

*10 soft flour tortillas*
*1 pound lean ground beef*
*1 envelope taco spices*
*2 cups shredded lettuce*
*1 cup chopped tomatoes*
*1 cup grated Monterey Jack cheese*
*picante or taco sauce to taste*
*sour cream (optional)*
*black olives, pitted and sliced*

*Makes 30 to 40*

- Using a 2½-inch round cookie cutter or a drinking glass turned upside-down, cut 3 or 4 small circles from each flour tortilla.
- In a skillet, brown ground beef. Drain off fat. Add taco spices and 1 cup water to beef. Mix thoroughly. Continue cooking over medium-low heat until juices begin to thicken.
- Cover tortilla rounds with shredded lettuce. Place one or two spoonfuls of meat atop each one. Add picante or taco sauce, to taste. Sprinkle with grated cheese. Add chopped tomato. If desired, top with a dollop of sour cream. Garnish with a small amount of sliced black olives.

# *Pork and Scallion Rolls*

*A sophisticated finger food*

- ½ *pound pork tenderloin, fat trimmed*
- 6-7 *scallions*
- 1 *clove garlic, minced*
- 1 *tablespoon soy sauce*
- 1 *tablespoon honey*
- 1 *tablespoon vegetable oil*
- 1 *tablespoon hoisin sauce*
- 1 *teaspoon freshly grated ginger root*

*Makes 20*

- Slice pork into 20 pieces. Flatten each slice with a knife.
- Trim roots and wilted leaves from scallions. Cut each into 3 or 4 pieces.
- Roll each pork slice around 1 scallion section. (Moisture in meat will keep it from unrolling.)
- In a small bowl, combine garlic, soy sauce, honey, vegetable oil, hoisin sauce, and ginger. Roll pork rolls in soy-honey mixture to coat.
- Place rolls in a shallow baking dish and bake at 400° for 15 minutes. Baste during baking. Serve hot or warm.

*Pork rolls can be covered and refrigerated before baking for up to 4 hours.*

# *Crab Won Tons*

*Surpasses all others*

- *8 ounces cream cheese, softened*
- *2 (6½ ounce) cans crabmeat, drained and cartilage removed*
- *⅓ cup chopped water chestnuts*
- *⅓ cup finely chopped scallions*
- *1 tablespoon soy sauce*
- *60 won ton wrappers*
- *1 egg, lightly beaten*
- *vegetable oil*

*Makes 60*

- Combine cream cheese, crabmeat, water chestnuts, scallions, and soy sauce. Place 1 teaspoon crabmeat mixture on each won ton wrapper. (Cover remaining wrappers with dampened towel to keep them pliable.) Brush top corner of won ton wrapper with egg. Fold bottom corner of won ton wrapper over filling to opposite corner, forming a triangle. Brush right corner of triangle with egg. Bring right and left corners together below filling; pinch corners to seal. Repeat with remaining won ton wrappers. (Cover filled won tons with dampened towel or plastic wrap to keep them from drying out.)
- Heat oil (1½ inches) in a 3-quart saucepan to medium high. Fry 8 won tons at a time, turning 2 or 3 times, until golden brown, about 3 minutes; drain.

*Fried won tons can be frozen for up to 1 month. To serve, heat frozen won tons uncovered in 400° oven for 10 to 12 minutes, or until hot.*

# *Herb and Mushroom Puff Pastries*

*A party-crowd pleaser*

- 1 *tablespoon minced shallots*
- 1 *tablespoon butter*
- 1/4 *pound fresh mushrooms, finely chopped*
- 1 *teaspoon lemon juice*
- 1 *teaspoon mixed dried herbs (any combination of dill, basil, tarragon, or oregano)*
- 3 1/2 *ounces garlic and herb cream cheese*
- 1/2 *pound frozen puff pastry*
- 1 *egg mixed with 1 tablespoon water (egg wash)*

*Makes 15*

- Sauté shallots in butter until soft, about 5 minutes.
- Add mushrooms and lemon juice. Cook until mushrooms are soft and juices absorbed. Add herbs. Mix well and set aside to cool.
- Mix cream cheese with cooled mushrooms. Season to taste.
- Roll out puff pastry into a 10x12-inch rectangle. Spread with filling and cut into fifteen 2x4-inch rectangles.
- Roll up each rectangle and brush with egg wash.
- Place seam-side down on an ungreased baking sheet. Bake at 350° for 15 minutes, or until golden.

*Herb mushroom rolls can be prepared ahead and frozen before baking.*

# *Filled Puffy Phyllo Triangles*

*Any one of these is sure to receive a standing ovation.*

*1 pound butter, melted*
*1 pound phyllo pastry dough*

## *Goat Cheese and Prosciutto Filling*

*3/4 pound goat cheese*
*2 eggs*
*1 cup heavy cream*
*1 teaspoon thyme*
*1/2 pound thinly sliced prosciutto, chopped*

## *Roquefort and Pistachio Filling*

*4 ounces Roquefort cheese*
*4 ounces cream cheese*
*1 egg*
*1/2 cup coarsely chopped, shelled pistachios*
*1/4 teaspoon nutmeg*

## *Spinach-Feta Filling*

*10 ounces frozen chopped spinach, defrosted and well-drained*
*1/2 cup finely chopped yellow onion, sautéed in 3 tablespoons oil*
*1/4 teaspoon nutmeg*
*1/2 cup finely chopped fresh dill or mint*
*1/3 cup ricotta cheese*
*1/4 cup crumbled feta cheese*

*Makes 100 appetizers*

- Combine ingredients for filling of your choice; set aside. Refrigerate if necessary.
- Unwrap phyllo onto a cutting surface, leaving it stacked. Cut into 4-inch strips. Work with phyllo strips a few at a time. Wrap remainder in a damp towel. Place one strip of dough on work surface. Using a pastry brush, spread strip evenly with butter. Take another strip, place on top of first; butter again.
- Place 1 tablespoon of filling at one end of buttered strip. Fold phyllo over filling in a triangle shape, as if folding a flag. Wrap end under; place on cookie sheet. Brush top with butter. Bake at 425° approximately 15 minutes, or until puffed and golden brown. Serve hot.

*Puffs can be frozen before baking. There is no need to defrost before cooking. Allow additional baking time.*

## *Vegetable Pizza*

*Here's one your teens will enjoy both making and eating.*

- *16 refrigerated crescent rolls*
- *12 ounces cream cheese*
- *¼ cup mayonnaise*
- *1 clove garlic, mashed*
- *½ teaspoon dill*
- *½ teaspoon chives*
- *assorted raw vegetables*
- *alfalfa sprouts*

- Unroll crescent rolls onto a 9x13-inch pan or a 14-inch round pizza pan. Bake according to package directions, or until lightly browned. Cool.
- Beat cream cheese, mayonnaise, and seasonings until well blended. Spread over baked rolls.
- Top with any combination of broccoli or cauliflower flowerets, grated carrots, sliced mushrooms, diced green pepper, diced tomatoes, and grated cheddar or colby cheese. Top with alfalfa sprouts.

## *Almond Cheese Pizza*

*This pizza will bring rave reviews.*

- *1 (10 inch) prepared pizza shell*
- *1 clove garlic, minced*
- *1½ tablespoons olive oil, divided*
- *¾ cup ricotta cheese*
- *½ cup grated mozzarella cheese*
- *½ cup grated fontina cheese*
- *4 tablespoons grated Parmesan cheese, divided*
- *2 ounces prosciutto, finely chopped*
- *¼ teaspoon dried basil*
- *¼ teaspoon oregano*
- *½ cup toasted, blanched, slivered almonds*

- Mix garlic with ½ teaspoon oil and brush dough with mixture.
- Spread ricotta on dough. Sprinkle with mozzarella, fontina, 2 tablespoons Parmesan, prosciutto, basil, and oregano. Lightly press almonds into toppings. Sprinkle with remaining Parmesan. Drizzle top with remaining oil. Bake at 425° for 20 to 25 minutes, or until crust is golden.

# *Three Pepper Pizza*

*Be creative...pesto, Brie, and sun-dried tomatoes will also elevate pizza to new heights of gastronomic pleasure.*

- 1/3 *cup each red, yellow, and green peppers, cut into 1/2-inch pieces*
- *olive oil*
- 8 *fresh mushrooms, sliced*
- *pizza dough*
- *cornmeal for pan*
- 1 *cup grated mozzarella cheese*
- 6 *slices prosciutto, cut into 1/2-inch pieces*
- 3/4 *cup pizza sauce with oregano*
- 1/3 *cup pitted and sliced black olives*
- 1/2 *cup grated Parmesan cheese*

- In a medium saucepan over low heat, cook peppers in 2 tablespoons oil until half done, about 10 minutes. Drain peppers on paper towels.
- In a bowl, lightly toss mushrooms with 1 teaspoon of oil until coated. Set aside.
- Roll out pizza dough on a floured surface. Lightly grease pizza pan with oil and sprinkle with cornmeal. Place dough in pizza pan and trim edges. Bake for 10 minutes at 425°. Remove from oven and lightly brush with oil. Sprinkle with half the mozzarella and all the sauce. Top with peppers, mushrooms, and olives. Sprinkle with remaining mozzarella and top with Parmesan. Bake on bottom oven rack for 20 minutes.

*Cut pizza in a grid-like pattern, not slices, to create bite-size morsels to offer as hors d'oeuvres.*

# *Caponata*

*Terrific in quantity for a large party*

- 2 *medium eggplants*
- 1 *large red pepper, cut into 1-inch squares*
- 1 *large yellow pepper, cut into 1-inch squares*
- 2 *medium zucchini, peeled and julienned*
- 2 *medium white onions, quartered and thinly sliced*
- ¼ *cup capers*
- ½ *cup pitted green olives*
- 1 *(15 ounce) can whole tomatoes, pureed*
- 1 *(15 ounce) can tomato sauce*
- 1 *tablespoon minced garlic*
- *salt and pepper*
- ⅔ *cup olive oil*
- ½ *cup white vinegar*
- 1 *tablespoon sugar*
- *fresh Italian parsley for garnish*
- *flat bread or thinly-sliced Italian bread*

*Serves 16 to 20*

- Peel eggplant and cut into 1-inch cubes. Put in a strainer and sprinkle with salt. Place heavy bowl on top to press out moisture. Drain for 30 minutes. Rinse thoroughly and dry on paper towels.
- In a large 11x15-inch roasting pan, combine eggplant, peppers, zucchini, onions, capers, olives, tomatoes, tomato sauce, garlic, and oil. Sprinkle lightly with salt and pepper. Mix thoroughly.
- Combine vinegar and sugar in a saucepan; heat until sugar dissolves. Pour over vegetables. Mix thoroughly. Bake in oven for 2 to 2½ hours, turning vegetables every ½ hour. Garnish with parsley and serve at room temperature with flat bread or thinly-sliced Italian bread.

*This recipe can be prepared 4 to 5 days in advance.*

# *French Bread Canapés*

*A tempting assortment for a large party*

*12 ½-inch thick slices French bread*

- Place bread slices under broiler until lightly browned, about 2 minutes. Brush untoasted side with one of the following spreads. Broil until golden.

## *Cheese Spread*

*½ cup grated Parmesan cheese*
*½ cup grated mozzarella cheese*
*3 tablespoons minced scallion*
*½ teaspoon dried Italian herb seasoning*
*¼ cup mayonnaise*

- Combine all ingredients, except tomatoes, in a medium bowl. Spread on prepared French bread. Garnish with sun-dried tomatoes.

## *Shrimp and Cheese Spread*

*5 ounces shrimp, cooked, peeled, deveined, and chopped*
*3 tablespoons minced scallion*
*¼ teaspoon garlic powder*
*3 tablespoons butter*
*2 tablespoons chopped fresh parsley*
*1 cup shredded mozzarella cheese*

- Sauté shrimp, scallion, and garlic powder in butter for 2 to 3 minutes. Stir in parsley. Combine cheese with shrimp and butter mixture. Spread on prepared French bread.

## *Jalapeño Spread*

*8 ounces cream cheese, softened*
*1 cup shredded Monterey Jack cheese*
*2 jalapeño peppers, seeded and finely chopped*
*1 sweet red pepper, seeded and finely chopped*

- Whip cream cheese with an electric mixer. By hand, mix in jalapeño, red pepper, and Monterey Jack cheese. Spread on prepared French bread.

## *Baked Brie Wedges*

*Irresistible!*

- *1 pound frozen puff pastry*
- *3/4 pound Brie cheese, cut into 24 slender wedges*
- *5 tablespoons butter, divided*
- *1 (6 ounce) jar raspberry jam*
- *juice of 1 lemon*

*Makes 24*

- Roll puff pastry to 1/8-inch thickness. Cut pastry into 4-inch squares.
- Roll Brie together with pastry, tucking in ends. Melt 4 tablespoons butter; brush over rolls. Bake at 350 ° for 20 minutes, or until lightly browned.
- Melt together raspberry jam, remaining tablespoon butter, and lemon juice. Serve alongside baked Brie wedges.

## *Grilled Gruyère Triangles*

*An elegant grilled cheese*

- *6 slices soft white bread*
- *butter for spreading*
- *Dijon mustard*
- *1/4 pound Gruyère cheese, thinly sliced*
- *6 slices prosciutto or Virginia ham, sliced extremely thin*

*Makes 24*

- Butter bread and lay half the slices butter-side down on work surface. Spread unbuttered side with a little mustard and cover with cheese. Add prosciutto. Top with remaining bread to form a sandwich with butter on outside. Heat a heavy skillet or griddle and fry sandwiches slowly until golden and cheese has melted. Trim crusts and cut each sandwich into 8 triangles. Serve immediately.

*If preparing these for a crowd, place sandwiches on a baking sheet. Bake at 425° for 10 minutes. Turn; bake an additional 5 minutes.*

## *Mozzarella Marinara*

*Second to Lambchop, this is Shari Lewis' favorite.*

- *1 pound mozzarella cheese, cut into ½-inch slices*
- *½ cup flour*
- *2 eggs, lightly beaten*
- *1 cup herbed and seasoned bread crumbs*
- *olive oil*
- *1 cup pizza sauce or homemade tomato sauce*

*Makes 16*

- Dip each slice of cheese into egg, then flour, then back into egg, and finally into bread crumbs. Pack bread crumbs against surface of cheese to form a good crust.
- Place slices on a plate and freeze for 20 minutes, or refrigerate for 1 hour.
- Pour olive oil into a frying pan to a ¼-inch depth. When oil is very hot, add cold cheese slices. Brown crisply on each side. When cheese slices are crisp and just beginning to ooze through crust, lift carefully out of pan. Place on paper towels to drain.
- Serve warm with heated pizza sauce for dipping.

## *Black Olive Canapés*

*So easy...so good!*

- *1½ cups minced black olives*
- *½ cup mayonnaise*
- *2 tablespoons minced onion*
- *¼ teaspoon curry powder*
- *1 cup grated sharp cheddar cheese*
- *pita bread triangles*

*Makes 24*

- Combine all ingredients except pita bread. Spread mixture on bread triangles. Place under broiler for 3 to 4 minutes, or until bubbly. Serve hot.

*Spread can be made ahead and refrigerated or frozen for a short period of time.*

# *Mix 'N' Match Vegetable Hors d'Oeuvres*

*Fresh peapods, cherry tomatoes, cucumber rounds, endive, or oval carrot slices can serve as beautifully edible holders for these delicious fillings. Consider the possibilities!*

## *Salmon Cream Filling*

- *½ pound fresh salmon fillet*
- *1 teaspoon dill*
- *1 cup heavy cream, whipped*
- *white pepper*

• Poach salmon with dill for approximately 10 minutes, or until fish is tender and flakes easily with a fork. Mash salmon and mix with whipped cream until well blended. Season to taste. Pipe onto prepared vegetable holders using a pastry bag, or serve as a first course in hollowed-out lemon halves.

## *Tabouli Filling*

- *⅓ cup cracked wheat*
- *2 small tomatoes, skinned, seeded and chopped*
- *½ green pepper, seeded and chopped*
- *1 shallot, minced*
- *1 tablespoon chopped fresh mint*
- *1 tablespoon minced parsley or cilantro*
- *2 tablespoons olive oil*
- *lemon juice*

• Soak cracked wheat in cold water for 1 hour. Drain well, wrap in a towel, and squeeze out all excess moisture. Spread wheat on a tray to dry. Put all prepared vegetables in a mixing bowl with soaked wheat; add mint, parsley, and oil. Season well with salt, pepper, and lemon juice. Spoon tabouli onto vegetable holders.

## *Seasoned Cheese Filling*

- *4 ounces garlic and herb cream cheese*
- *3 ounces cream cheese*
- *2 tablespoons heavy cream*

• Blend softened cheeses together with cream until mixture has reached the proper consistency for piping. Place in a pastry bag fitted with a decorator tip and pipe onto vegetable holders.

## *New Potatoes with Sour Cream and Bacon*

*You can't go wrong.*

- *20 very small new potatoes*
- *1 cup sour cream*
- *8 slices bacon, crisply fried and chopped*

*Makes 40*

- Boil potatoes until tender, about 15 minutes.
- Cut potatoes in half; rest flat side on a cutting board. With a small melon baller, scoop out a small hole on top side of potato.
- Fill hole with sour cream and sprinkle with bacon.

*Fresh chives or caviar can be substituted for bacon.*

## *Presto Pesto Boats*

*The name says it all.*

- *1 package finger rolls (Parker House rolls)*
- *3 tablespoons butter, melted*
- *8 ounces fresh spinach, rinsed, drained, and stemmed*
- *½ cup pecans*
- *⅓ cup grated Parmesan cheese*
- *2 cloves garlic*
- *2 tablespoons olive oil*
- *¼ teaspoon salt*
- *thin red bell pepper strips for garnish*

*Makes 24*

- Cut rolls lengthwise from top to bottom. Using fingers, pull soft bread from cut side of each, leaving a crust shell or "boat" about ⅜-inch thick. Brush insides of boats with melted butter. Bake at 400° on a cookie sheet until crisp and golden.
- Add spinach to food processor or blender in batches, processing after each addition until finely chopped. Add pecans, Parmesan, garlic, olive oil, and salt; process until smooth.
- Spoon pesto into toasted boats. Garnish with red pepper.

# *Crudités and Dips*

*Complement your offering of fresh vegetables with a variety of homemade dips.*

## *Crudités*

*blanched asparagus*
*red, green, or yellow pepper wedges*
*broccoli flowerets*
*cauliflower flowerets*
*peapods*
*scallions*
*black olives*
*endive*
*cherry tomatoes*
*carrot spears*
*zucchini spears*
*cheese strips*

*For an all-natural presentation, hollow out a leafy cabbage or several nicely-formed peppers to use as serving bowls for the following dips.*

## *Fresh Dill Dip*

- 2 *cups sour cream*
- 1½ *cups mayonnaise*
- 6 *tablespoons fresh dill*
- ½ *small onion, minced*
- 2 *tablespoons Beau Monde*
- 3 *tablespoons minced fresh parsley*

• Mix all ingredients. Cover and refrigerate.

## *Honey Mustard Dip*

- 1 *jar sharp and creamy mustard*
- ½-¾ *cup mayonnaise*
- ¼ *cup honey*

• Combine all ingredients. Mix until smooth.

## *Crudités and Dips, continued*

### *Water Chestnut Dip*

*1 small onion*
*3 tablespoons fresh parsley*
*1 can water chestnuts, drained*
*1 tablespoon candied ginger*
*2 cloves garlic*
*1 cup mayonnaise*
*1 cup sour cream*
*1 tablespoon soy sauce*
*dash of salt*

- Place onion, parsley, water chestnuts, candied ginger, and garlic into a food processor bowl. Process until finely chopped.
- In a mixing bowl, combine mayonnaise, sour cream, chopped ingredients, soy sauce, and salt.

### *Curry Dip*

*1½ cups mayonnaise*
*3 tablespoons ketchup*
*3 tablespoons grated onion*
*3 tablespoons honey*
*1 tablespoon lemon juice*
*1 tablespoon curry powder*

- Combine all ingredients. Mix until smooth.

### *Shrimp Dip*

*8 ounces cream cheese*
*¼ cup chili sauce*
*2 teaspoons lemon juice*
*1 tablespoon milk*
*1 teaspoon chopped onion*
*1 tablespoon horseradish*
*salt and pepper*
*½ pound cooked shrimp, minced*

- Combine all ingredients and mix well.

# *Baked Dips*

*When the dips are as marvelous as those that follow, family and company alike are sure to be pleased.*

## *Dippers*

*sliced French bread*
*rye cubes*
*flat bread*
*seasoned breadsticks*
*English water crackers*
*corn chips*

*Hollowed out loaves of bread, especially dark, round ones, offer another way to serve several of these baked dips.*

## *Cheese Ramekin*

*1 cup mayonnaise*
*1 cup grated sharp cheddar cheese*
*½ cup grated onion*
*½ cup chopped broccoli flowerets*

- Combine ingredients and mix well. Bake in a soufflé dish at 350° for 30 minutes.

## *Hot Clam Melt*

*3 (6 ounce) cans clams*
*16 ounces cream cheese*
*¼ cup clam juice*
*¼ cup minced onion*
*1 tablespoon Worcestershire sauce*
*2 tablespoons lemon juice*
*bottled hot pepper sauce to taste*
*freshly ground pepper to taste*

- Combine ingredients and mix well. Place in a small casserole or ramekin. Bake at 250° for 1 hour.

## *Baked Dips, continued*

### *Sherried Crab and Lobster*

- *16 ounces cream cheese, softened*
- *1 cup sour cream*
- *4 tablespoons mayonnaise*
- *½ teaspoon lemon juice*
- *1 teaspoon dry mustard*
- *2 dashes garlic salt or powder*
- *3 tablespoons sherry*
- *8 ounces cooked lobster meat*
- *8 ounces fresh crabmeat*
- *4 ounces shredded cheddar cheese*

- Blend all ingredients except crab, lobster, and half the cheddar cheese in a food processor.
- Fold in crab and lobster and put in an oven-proof serving dish. Top with remaining cheddar. Bake at 325° for 45 minutes.

### *Reuben Dip*

- *1 cup sauerkraut, rinsed and drained*
- *1 tablespoon butter*
- *2 scallions, sliced*
- *1½ cups shredded Monterey Jack cheese*
- *4 ounces cream cheese, cubed*
- *2 tablespoons ketchup*
- *2 teaspoons Dijon mustard*
- *¼ teaspoon pepper*
- *½ pound corned beef, chopped*

- Sauté scallions in butter until soft. Stir in cheese, cream cheese, ketchup, mustard, and pepper. Cook over low heat until cheeses have melted. Add corned beef. Pour mixture on top of sauerkraut in a small casserole dish. Bake at 350° for 10 to 15 minutes. Stir before serving.

# *Fruit and Dips*

*These unusual but sweetly scrumptious dips are perfect with the freshest fruits of the season.*

## *Fresh Fruit*

*pineapple chunks*
*melon wedges*
*whole strawberries or grapes*
*kiwi fruit slices*

*A hollowed out pineapple is the perfect vessel for serving any of these fruit dips.*

## *Kahlúa Dip*

*8 ounces cream cheese*
*1 cup heavy cream, whipped*
*3/4 cup firmly packed brown sugar*
*3-6 ounces unsalted peanuts, finely chopped*
*1/3 cup Kahlúa*

- Combine all ingredients. Refrigerate at least 4 hours before serving.

## *Ginger Lime Dip*

*1/2 cup mayonnaise*
*1/2 cup sour cream*
*2 teaspoons grated lime peel*
*1 tablespoon fresh lime juice*
*1 tablespoon honey*
*1/2 teaspoon ginger*

- Combine all ingredients and mix well. Serve chilled.

## *Pecan Fruit Dip*

*8 ounces cream cheese*
*1 cup firmly packed brown sugar*
*1/2 cup chopped pecans*

- Combine all ingredients and mix well.

# *Sparkling Sangria*

*There's a "secret" ingredient here to make your Sangria the Grandest of them all.*

*1 (750 ml) bottle red wine*
*¼ cup Grand Marnier*
*1 tablespoon fresh lemon juice*
*1 tablespoon sugar*
*1 orange, thinly sliced*
*1 lemon, thinly sliced*
*1 lime, thinly sliced*
*1 cup lemon-lime soda*

*Serves 4*

- Combine wine, Grand Marnier, lemon juice, sugar, and fruit in a large glass pitcher. (This portion of the recipe can be prepared up to 24 hours before serving.) Keep refrigerated. When ready to serve, add soda and ice.

# *White Sangria*

*A simple change — from red to white — creates a drink that's always right!*

*1 (750 ml) bottle dry white wine*
*½ cup Curaçao*
*¼ cup sugar*
*1 orange, thinly sliced*
*1 lemon, thinly sliced*
*1 lime, thinly sliced*
*4-5 strawberries, sliced*
*1 cup club soda*

*Serves 4*

- Combine wine, Curaçao, and sugar in a large pitcher. Stir until sugar is dissolved.
- Add sliced fruits. Cover and chill in refrigerator at least 1 hour.
- Just before serving, add soda and ice.

# *Kir with Ice Garland*

*Imagine this at your next shower or very special event.*

*Kir*

- *2 (1.5 liter) bottles dry white wine*
- *1 cup Crème de Cassis*
- *1 liter club soda*

*Ice Garland*

- *6-8 whole strawberries*
- *1 lemon, sliced into rounds*
- *4-6 pink sweetheart roses*
- *sprigs of fresh mint*
- *water*

*Serves 10 to 12*

- *Kir* — Combine all ingredients in a large punch bowl. Float ice garland on top.
- *Ice Garland* — Fill a ring mold half full with water. Freeze to slushy stage. Attractively arrange strawberries, lemon, roses, and mint. Carefully add water to top of ring. Freeze. When ready to serve, release ice garland from ring mold.

*For a particularly festive occasion, prepare "Kir Royale" by substituting champagne for wine.*

# *Indian Summer Punch*

*A celebration of citrus*

- *2 cups orange juice*
- *¼ cup fresh lime juice*
- *¼ cup fresh lemon juice*
- *2 tablespoons superfine sugar*
- *1 cup vodka*
- *fresh fruit slices for garnish*

*Serves 8*

- Stir juices and sugar in a tall pitcher until sugar dissolves. Add vodka and mix well. Serve over ice.

## *Welcoming Wassail*

*The finest winter holiday drink ever to grace your punch bowl*

- *4 cups apple cider*
- *½ cup firmly packed dark brown sugar*
- *½ cup dark rum*
- *¼ cup brandy*
- *2 tablespoons Grand Marnier, divided*
- *¼ teaspoon cinnamon*
- *¼ teaspoon cloves*
- *⅛ teaspoon allspice*
- *½ lemon, thinly sliced*
- *½ orange, thinly sliced*
- *1 cup heavy cream*
- *2 tablespoons confectioner's sugar*
- *freshly grated nutmeg*

*Serves 8 to 10*

- Whip heavy cream together with confectioner's sugar until soft peaks form. Flavor with 1 tablespoon Grand Marnier. Set aside in refrigerator.
- Heat apple cider and brown sugar together in a large saucepan to a boil. Stir until sugar dissolves. Remove from heat.
- Add rum, brandy, and 1 tablespoon Grand Marnier. Stir in spices. Add lemon and orange slices. Heat over medium heat, stirring 2 minutes. Do not boil.
- Pour into wine glasses. Top each glass with flavored whipped cream and freshly grated nutmeg.

# *Perfect Punch*

*This punch is perfectly easy, perfectly delicious, and perfectly pretty.*

- *3 (6 ounce) cans frozen orange juice concentrate*
- *3 (6 ounce) cans frozen lemonade concentrate*
- *6 (6 ounce) cans water*
- *1 (46 ounce) can pineapple juice*
- *1 (10 ounce) package frozen sweetened strawberries, thawed*
- *1 (2 liter) bottle ginger ale, lemon-lime soda, or club soda*
- *½ gallon fruit sherbet*

*Serves 24 to 30*

- Purée orange juice and lemonade concentrates in a blender with water. Pour into a large container. Add pineapple juice. Purée frozen strawberries and combine with other juices. (This portion of recipe can be prepared ahead of time and refrigerated.)

- When ready to serve, pour half the juice mixture into a punch bowl. Add half the sherbet. Finally, pour in half the soda. Stir gently and serve. (When punch bowl is empty, repeat with remaining ingredients.)

# *Creamsicle Punch*

*This is just as yummy with frozen yogurt.*

- *1 (6 ounce) can frozen orange juice concentrate*
- *1 teaspoon vanilla*
- *2 large scoops vanilla ice cream*
- *½ cup sugar*
- *6 ice cubes*

- Whip all ingredients together in a blender. Serve immediately.

*Serves 4*

# *Kids' Colada*

*Both the young and the young-at-heart will be tempted by this scrumptious non-alcoholic punch.*

- *2 cups cream of coconut*
- *6 cups pineapple juice, chilled*
- *3 cups ginger ale, chilled*

- In a punch bowl, stir cream of coconut and pineapple juice until mixed. Add ginger ale, stirring gently. Serve immediately.

*Serves 8 to 10*

## *Mocha Irish Cream*

*This will keep for two months, but we guarantee it will be gone long before that!*

- *1 tablespoon chocolate syrup*
- *1 teaspoon instant coffee (not freeze dried)*
- *1 pint heavy cream*
- *1 (14 ounce) can sweetened condensed milk*
- *1 cup rye whiskey*

- Place chocolate syrup and instant coffee in a blender and process for 3 minutes.
- Combine cream and condensed milk in a large bowl. Add chocolate mixture. Rinse blender container with whiskey, then add whiskey to other ingredients. Stir. Keep refrigerated.

*Serves 4*

## *Frozen Margaritas*

*Keep a batch of these margaritas at-the-ready in your freezer. Because of the low freezing point of alcohol, they will remain perfectly slushy.*

- *2 cups tequila*
- *1 cup Triple Sec*
- *4 cups margarita mix*
- *3 cups water*

- Combine all ingredients and freeze. Stir before scooping into chilled glasses.

*Serves 18 to 20*

# SOUPS & SALADS

# SOUPS & SALADS



*Chilled Soups*



*Hot Soups*



*Hearty Soups*



*Main Dish Salads*



*Vegetable Salads*



*Potato, Rice, and Pasta Salads*



*Molded Salads*



*Dressings*

## Chilled Cucumber Soup

*For a special presentation, serve this soup in frosted wine glasses.*

- *2 cups chicken stock*
- *3 cucumbers, peeled, sliced, and seeds removed*
- *1 tablespoon chopped onion*
- *1 teaspoon snipped fresh dill (or 1/2 teaspoon dried)*
- *salt and pepper*
- *2 cups plain yogurt*
- *1/2 cup finely chopped walnuts or pecans*

- In a saucepan, combine stock, cucumbers, and onion. Bring to a boil. Reduce heat and simmer until cucumbers are just tender, about 5 to 7 minutes. Cool.
- In a food processor or blender, purée soup, dill, salt, and pepper until smooth. Add yogurt and nuts. Chill.
- Serve cold. Garnish with sliced cucumbers.

*Serves 6*

## Minted Melon Soup

*This soup says summer.*

- *1/2 honeydew, rind removed, diced*
- *1 cantaloupe, rind removed, diced*
- *1 fresh pineapple, cored and chopped*
- *1 cup pineapple juice*
- *1 cup sparkling water*
- *1 tablespoon chopped fresh mint*

- Place all fruits in a food processor or blender; process until puréed. If necessary, do in batches.
- Combine puréed fruits and remaining ingredients in a large bowl. Chill at least 3 hours.

*This is beautiful when served in halved cantaloupe or honeydew bowls.*

*Serves 4*

# *Iced Gazpacho*

*A refreshing chilled treat after tennis*

- *2 cups tomato juice*
- *1 cup peeled and chopped tomatoes*
- *1 small green pepper, finely chopped*
- *1 small cucumber, peeled and finely chopped*
- *3 celery stalks, finely chopped*
- *1 small onion, finely chopped*
- *1 clove garlic, minced*
- *2 tablespoons red wine vinegar*
- *2 tablespoons olive oil*
- *1 teaspoon salt*
- *½ teaspoon Worcestershire sauce*
- *¼ teaspoon pepper*

*Serves 8*

- Combine all ingredients in a blender or food processor. Whirl until mixed thoroughly.
- Chill until ready to serve.

# *Berry Pink Strawberry Soup*

*Pretty and pink—a beautiful beginning to any luncheon*

- *1 pint fresh (or 16 ounces unsweetened frozen) whole strawberries*
- *1 cup sour cream*
- *1 cup light cream*
- *¼ cup sugar*
- *2 tablespoons white wine*

*Serves 8*

- Process strawberries in a blender. Add remaining ingredients and blend well.
- Chill overnight.
- Garnish with one large perfect strawberry.

# *Confetti Soup*

*Festive and flavorful*

- 4-6 *slices of bacon, crisply fried and crumbled*
- 2 *tablespoons olive oil*
- 1 *small onion, chopped*
- 2-3 *carrots, julienned*
- 1 *small sweet red pepper, julienned*
- 2 *spinach leaves, shredded*
- 6 *cups chicken broth*
- 8 *ounces cooked cheese tortellini*

*Serves 6*

- Heat olive oil in a stock pot; lightly sauté onion, carrots, and red pepper. Add chicken broth to sauteed vegetables and simmer 10 minutes.
- Add shredded spinach and tortellini. Simmer 5 minutes.
- Add cooked bacon just before serving.

*When served with warm French bread, it's a meal in itself.*

# *Clear Mushroom Soup*

*Using wild rice will transform this simple recipe into a company classic.*

- 2 *tablespoons butter*
- 6 *large fresh mushrooms, sliced*
- 3 *tablespoons thinly sliced scallions*
- 4 *cups homemade beef stock or beef consomme*
- 1 *cup cooked rice*
- ½ *cup sherry*
- *freshly ground pepper*

*Serves 4 to 6*

- Heat butter in a stock pot. Cook mushrooms until lightly browned. Add beef stock, rice, and scallions. Heat for 5 minutes. If using homemade stock, be sure to bring soup to a boil.
- Add sherry and season with freshly ground pepper.

## *Pumpkin Bisque*

*Serve in a pumpkin shell for a perfect harvest setting.*

- *2 tablespoons butter*
- *1 tablespoon chopped scallion*
- *1 (16 ounce) can cooked pumpkin or 1½ cups cooked, mashed pumpkin*
- *1 cup chicken broth*
- *2 teaspoons brown sugar*
- *2 cups light cream*
- *½ teaspoon salt*
- *⅛ teaspoon white pepper*
- *⅛ teaspoon cinnamon*

*Serves 4 to 6*

- In a saucepan, sauté scallion in butter until transparent (do not brown). Stir in remaining ingredients, except cream; bring to a boil and simmer 5 minutes. Thin with cream to desired consistency.

*Select a perfect 6 to 7 pound pumpkin with a flat bottom. Neatly remove top and pulp. (Seedless meat can be used for soup.) Coat inside with soft butter; pour prepared soup into pumpkin. Place on a cookie sheet. Keep warm in 175° oven until ready to serve.*

## *Zucchini Yogurt Soup*

*Healthy, delicious, and "micro" quick...*

- *2 tablespoons margarine*
- *1 medium onion, chopped*
- *2 medium potatoes, thinly sliced*
- *1 pound zucchini, thinly sliced*
- *3 cups chicken broth*
- *2 tablespoons lemon juice*
- *¼ cup chopped fresh parsley*
- *½ teaspoon salt*
- *¼ teaspoon pepper*
- *1 cup plain yogurt*
- *¼ cup chopped chives or scallions*

*Serves 4 to 6*

- In a 3-quart microwave casserole, combine margarine and onion. Microwave on high 2 to 3 minutes. Add potatoes. Cover tightly. Cook on high 6 to 8 minutes, stirring once. Stir in zucchini, cover, and cook on high 4 to 6 minutes more, stirring once.
- Spoon mixture into a blender and purée. Return to casserole; add broth, lemon juice, parsley, salt, and pepper. Cover and microwave on high 6 to 8 minutes, stirring once.
- Serve in bowls and top with a dollop of yogurt and chives.

# *Classic French Onion Soup*

*Adds elegance to any dinner*

- *4 large onions, thinly sliced*
- *1 tablespoon butter*
- *1 tablespoon vegetable oil*
- *1/4 teaspoon sugar*
- *2 tablespoons flour*
- *6 cups beef broth, heated*
- *1/4 cup dry white wine*
- *salt and pepper to taste*
- *4 slices French bread, 1/2-inch thick*
- *2 teaspoons vegetable oil*
- *1 clove garlic, peeled and cut*
- *2 tablespoons cognac*
- *1 cup grated Swiss cheese*

*Serves 4*

- In a covered 4-quart saucepan, cook onions over low heat with butter and oil for 15 minutes. Stir occasionally. Uncover; increase heat to moderate. Add sugar. Continue cooking; stir frequently until onions turn golden brown. Sprinkle onions with flour; stir over heat for 2 to 3 minutes. Blend in hot broth and wine; season to taste. Simmer partially covered for one hour.
- Prepare bread slices by baking in a 350° oven for 15 minutes. Baste each slice with ½ teaspoon of oil and rub with a garlic clove. Continue cooking for an additional 15 minutes, or until lightly toasted.
- Before serving, add cognac to soup. Pour soup into 4 ovenproof bowls. Sprinkle 1 or 2 tablespoons of cheese into each bowl. Float French bread on top of soup; sprinkle with remaining cheese.
- Bake at 325° for 15 to 20 minutes. Broil for 2 to 3 minutes until cheese is golden.

# *Autumn Bisque*

*This soup looks, smells, and tastes like fall.*

- *1/4 cup butter*
- *3/4 cup minced yellow onion*
- *4 ounces sliced fresh mushrooms*
- *1 pound carrots, peeled and sliced*
- *1 pound parsnips, peeled and sliced*
- *1 apple, peeled and sliced*
- *3 cups chicken stock*
- *6 sprigs fresh thyme*
- *1 1/2 cups light cream*
- *1/2 cup apple cider*
- *1/4 teaspoon nutmeg*
- *salt and pepper to taste*

*Serves 6*

- In a large skillet, melt butter; add onions and mushrooms. Sauté over medium heat until soft, about 10 minutes. Place carrots, parsnips, apple, onion, and mushrooms in a large pot. Add chicken stock and thyme. Bring contents to a boil. Cover, simmer, and cook for 30 minutes, or until vegetables are soft.
- Let soup cool slightly. Remove and discard woody stems of thyme.
- Pour soup into a food processor or blender and purée until smooth. Return soup to pot. Add cream, cider, and nutmeg. Reheat slowly until soup is warm. Season to taste. Thin bisque to desired consistency with additional cream or cider.

# *Cream of Broccoli Soup with Croutons*

*A great basic with a clever crouton twist*

- 2½ *pounds broccoli*
- ½ *cup chopped onion*
- ¾ *cup chopped celery*
- ¾ *teaspoon salt*
- ½ *teaspoon pepper*
- ½ *teaspoon nutmeg*
- 2 *bay leaves*
- 1½ *cups water*
- 3 *(14 ounce) cans chicken broth*
- ¼ *cup butter*
- 4 *tablespoons flour*
- 3 *cups light cream*

*Serves 12 to 16*

- Cut stems from broccoli. Combine broccoli flowerets, onion, celery, seasonings, water, and broth in a large stock pot. Bring to a boil and simmer about 30 minutes. Drain, reserving broth.

- Remove bay leaves. Purée vegetables in a blender with 1 cup of broth.

- In a stock pot, melt butter; add flour, stir until smooth. Add reserved broth, puréed vegetables, and light cream; stir until hot and thickened.

*For a festive touch, use seasonal cookie cutters to create shapes from thin slices of bread. Brush them lightly with butter before toasting in 325° oven until lightly browned. Sprinkle with grated Parmesan cheese. Float on soup and serve.*

# *Creative Carrot Soup*

*A beautiful beginning to a special meal*

- 2 *pounds carrots, peeled or scrubbed, and chopped*
- 4 *cups chicken stock*
- 1½ *teaspoons salt*
- 1 *cup chopped onion*
- 2 *small cloves garlic*
- ⅓ *cup chopped almonds*
- 3-4 *tablespoons butter*
- 1 *cup heavy cream*
- 1 *teaspoon thyme*
- 1 *teaspoon marjoram*
- 1 *teaspoon basil*
- 1 *teaspoon ginger*
- *dash of sherry (to be added to each serving)*

*Serves 4 to 6*

- Bring carrots, stock, and salt to a boil. Cover and simmer 15 minutes. Cool to room temperature.
- Sauté onion, garlic, and almonds in butter until onion is translucent.
- Purée carrot mixture and onion mixture together in a blender or food processor until smooth. Return the purée to a saucepan. Whisk in heavy cream. Heat very slowly. Season with thyme, marjoram, basil, and ginger.
- Add a dash of sherry to each serving.

*Create a carrot garnish using tiny baby carrots and sprigs of fresh parsley for carrot greens.*

## *Sherried Brie Soup*

*A rich and elegant soup*

- *2½ pounds Brie cheese, crust removed*
- *1 quart chicken stock or broth*
- *2 tablespoons butter*
- *1 cup sliced fresh mushrooms*
- *1 cup julienned carrots*
- *½ cup sliced scallions*
- *¼ cup dry sherry*
- *2 cups heavy cream*
- *salt and pepper to taste*

*Serves 4*

- Dissolve Brie in hot chicken broth; strain.
- Melt butter over low heat. Add vegetables and sauté until tender. Add cheese mixture. Stir in cream, sherry, and seasonings.

## *Leek and Asparagus Bisque*

*A local favorite for all four seasons*

- *3 large leeks, white part only, cleaned thoroughly*
- *2 tablespoons olive oil*
- *2 tablespoons butter*
- *2 cups asparagus, tender parts only*
- *1 cup chicken stock*
- *1 cup heavy cream*
- *salt and pepper to taste*

*Serves 4 to 6*

- Sauté leeks in olive oil and butter until soft. Steam or boil asparagus. Add asparagus to leeks. Add chicken stock and heat thoroughly.
- Use a blender or food processor to cream ingredients. Add heavy cream, warm, and serve.

*For a festive garnish, save the long green portion of leeks. Tie these fronds to your soup bowl handle before putting soup into bowls.*

# *Seafood Bisque*

*A showcase for the stars of the sea...*

- 2 *slices lemon*
- 1 *small carrot, chopped*
- 1 *celery stalk, chopped (top reserved)*
- ¼ *teaspoon peppercorns*
- 2½ *cups water*
- 2 *teaspoons instant chicken bouillon granules*
- 4 *ounces salmon steak, cut ½-inch thick, or 4 ounces salmon fillet*
- 4 *ounces sea scallops, halved*
- ¾ *cup sliced scallions*
- 2 *tablespoons finely chopped shallots or onion*
- ½ *cup finely chopped celery*
- 3 *tablespoons butter*
- ¼ *cup flour*
- ¼ *teaspoon salt*
- 2 *tablespoons tomato paste*
- 2 *cups light cream*

*Serves 6 to 8*

- Combine lemon, carrot, celery top, and peppercorns in a cheesecloth bag. Place in a 2-quart saucepan with water and bouillon granules. Bring to a boil. Reduce heat, cover, and simmer 5 minutes.
- Add salmon. Return to a boil, cover, and simmer 3 minutes. Add scallops. Simmer 2 to 3 minutes longer, or until salmon flakes and scallops are opaque. Remove bag. Remove fish and scallops from poaching liquid using a slotted spoon. Strain liquid, reserving 2 cups; discard the remainder. Flake salmon, discarding bone and skin. Set salmon and scallops aside.
- In a large saucepan, cook scallions, shallots, and chopped celery in butter until vegetables are tender. Stir in flour and salt. Add reserved broth and tomato paste. Cook and stir until mixture is thickened and bubbly; cook and stir 1 minute more. Add flaked salmon, scallops, and light cream. (If making ahead, stop at this point, cover and chill.) Cook, stirring frequently, until heated through. Do not boil.

# *Holiday Eve Seafood Chowder*

*When a big holiday meal is planned for the next day, serve this chowder to your arriving family and guests the night before.*

- *1/4 cup butter, melted*
- *1 small onion, minced*
- *2 cups chicken broth*
- *1 cup chopped celery*
- *1 cup thinly sliced carrots*
- *salt and pepper to taste*
- *1 bay leaf*
- *1/2 teaspoon thyme*
- *1/2 pound haddock, cut into bite-size pieces*
- *3 cups milk*
- *1/4 cup flour*
- *1 cup heavy cream*
- *1/2 pound cooked shrimp*
- *1/2 pound poached scallops*
- *6 slices bacon, crisply fried*

*Serves 6 to 8*

- Sauté onion in butter until tender. Add broth, celery, carrots, salt, pepper, bay leaf, and thyme. Bring to a boil and simmer gently 10 to 15 minutes. Add haddock and simmer gently 10 minutes, or until fish flakes easily.
- Make a smooth paste by mixing 1 cup milk with flour. Add to hot mixture; cook and stir until mixture thickens.
- Add remaining milk, cream, shrimp, and scallops. Heat soup thoroughly, but do not boil.
- Add bacon just before serving.

*For an economical meal, 4 cans of drained clams can be substituted.*

# *Mulligatawny Soup*

*When you want to treat your family like company, serve them this special soup.*

- *2 tablespoons vegetable oil*
- *1/2 cup chopped onion*
- *2 teaspoons curry powder*
- *2 cups chicken broth*
- *1 1/2 cups water*
- *1/3 cup uncooked long-grain white rice*
- *1/2 teaspoon salt*
- *1/8 teaspoon pepper*
- *2 cups diced, cooked chicken*
- *1 cup unsweetened applesauce*
- *1/4 cup chopped fresh parsley*
- *1/2 cup heavy cream*

*Serves 4*

- Heat oil in a large saucepan. Add onion and curry; stir over medium-low heat 3 minutes, or until onion is translucent.
- Add chicken broth, water, rice, salt, and pepper. Bring to a boil. Reduce heat, cover, and simmer 20 minutes, or until rice is cooked.
- Stir in chicken, applesauce, and parsley. Cover and simmer 5 minutes, or until soup is hot. Remove from heat; stir in cream. Serve immediately.

# *Bountiful Beef Soup*

*A thick soup that is so substantial only a light dessert is needed to complete the meal*

### *Stock*

- *2 pounds beef shank*
- *2 quarts water*
- *1 onion, coarsely chopped*
- *1 carrot, coarsely chopped*
- *1 rib celery, top reserved*
- *1 sprig parsley*
- *1 bay leaf*
- *1 tablespoon salt*
- *1/4 teaspoon peppercorns*

### *Soup*

- *beef stock from above recipe*
- *3 tablespoons vegetable oil*
- *4 cups chopped vegetables (onion, carrot, and/or celery)*
- *1 pound escarole or spinach, rinsed and torn in pieces*
- *1/4 cup barley*
- *1 (16 ounce) can whole tomatoes*

*Serves 6 to 8*

- *The Stock* — Combine all ingredients for broth in a large saucepan. Bring to a boil. Cover and simmer 2 hours. Strain. Cut meat from bones and add to soup. Discard bones.
- *The Soup* — Heat oil in a large skillet and sauté vegetables 10 minutes, or until crisp-tender. Add escarole; cover and steam over low heat 10 minutes. Add remaining ingredients; simmer 45 minutes.

*Broth can be made ahead and kept frozen.*

# *Cheese Potato Soup*

*A stick-to-the ribs classic*

- 5-6 *Russet potatoes, peeled and cut into ½-inch cubes*
- *chicken broth or water to cover potatoes*
- 5 *tablespoons butter, divided*
- 2 *large yellow onions, thinly sliced*
- 2 *bay leaves*
- 1 *teaspoon dill*
- 1 *large clove garlic, minced*
- 2 *tablespoons flour*
- 2 *cups milk*
- 6 *ounces Swiss cheese, grated*
- 1 *tablespoon paprika*
- 1 *tablespoon Worcestershire sauce*
- *salt and pepper to taste*

*Serves 6*

- Boil potatoes in water or broth until tender. Do not discard cooking liquid.
- While potatoes are cooking, melt 3 tablespoons butter in a large, deep skillet. Add onions and bay leaves; sauté until onions are golden, stirring often. Add dill and garlic. Add contents of skillet to cooked potatoes.
- In skillet, melt remaining butter. Stir in flour and cook for 2 to 3 minutes. Add milk using a whisk to blend. Stir until thickened. Add cheese and stir until melted. Add mixture to potatoes.
- Stir in Worcestershire sauce, salt, pepper, and paprika. Heat soup thoroughly, but do not boil. Remove bay leaves before serving.

# *Country Lentil Soup*

*A full-bodied soup for a January afternoon*

- *1½ cups lentils*
- *4 slices bacon*
- *1 cup sliced leeks*
- *½ cup chopped onion*
- *¼ cup chopped carrot*
- *¾ cup chopped green pepper*
- *¾ cup chopped fresh tomatoes*
- *3 tablespoons butter*
- *1 (10½ ounce) can condensed beef bouillon*
- *2 teaspoons salt*
- *2 tablespoons red wine vinegar*
- *1 tablespoon flour*

*Serves 4 to 6*

- Place lentils in 5 cups cold water in a large stockpot. Bring to a boil. Reduce heat, cover, and simmer 1 hour.
- Cut bacon into small pieces and sauté in a large skillet until crisp. Add leeks, onion, carrot, pepper, and tomatoes. Sauté over low heat about 5 minutes. Add to stockpot with lentils when lentils are done cooking.
- Melt butter in same skillet; remove from heat. Stir in flour until smooth; gradually stir in bouillon. Add salt and vinegar. Heat to boiling, stirring constantly. Add mixture to stockpot and simmer over low heat about 30 minutes.

# *Heritage Soup*

*Grandfather always threw in an extra handful of barley as this soup was simmering.*

- *1/4 cup pearl barley*
- *4 cups chicken broth*
- *8 tablespoons vegetable oil, divided*
- *2 medium onions, chopped*
- *1 clove garlic, minced*
- *4 cups finely chopped green cabbage*
- *4 tablespoons flour*
- *4 cups milk*
- *3 chicken-flavored bouillon cubes*
- *1/2 teaspoon celery seed*
- *chopped fresh parsley for garnish*

*Serves 6 to 8*

- Combine barley and broth in a large saucepan; cook barley until soft. In a separate skillet, sauté onions, garlic, and cabbage in 4 tablespoons oil until soft, but not brown.
- Combine flour, milk, bouillon cubes, celery seed, and remaining oil in a medium saucepan over low heat. Cook until bouillon cubes have dissolved completely. Add warmed liquid to broth. Stir in sautéed vegetables. Heat thoroughly.

# *Caesar Salad*

*This recipe comes from First Lady Barbara Bush. Why not try this for your "first family"?*

- *2-3 cloves garlic*
- *½ cup olive oil*
- *4 cups bread cubes*
- *assorted lettuce greens*
- *1 cup grated Parmesan cheese*
- *½ cup crumbled bleu cheese*
- *1 teaspoon salt*
- *½ teaspoon freshly ground pepper*
- *12 teaspoons olive oil*
- *1 egg*
- *7 tablespoons lemon juice*
- *2 tablespoons Worcestershire sauce*

- Cut garlic into quarters and let sit in ½ cup olive oil overnight (out of refrigerator).
- Put bread cubes into a shallow pan. Toast cubes in a 300° oven for 30 minutes until golden brown, turning once with a fork. After cooling, wrap in wax paper until needed.
- Sprinkle lettuce with Parmesan cheese, bleu cheese, salt, and pepper. Add olive oil (not the oil treated with garlic). Mix together one egg, lemon juice, and Worcestershire sauce. Pour over salad and toss.
- Flavor croutons with garlic and oil mixture. Add to salad just before serving.

# *Orange and Romaine Toss*

*A colorful combination of fruits and greens*

- *1 head romaine lettuce, torn*
- *3 kiwi fruits, peeled and sliced*
- *1 (11 ounce) can Mandarin orange sections, drained*
- *1 large red onion, sliced*
- *½ cup olive oil*
- *¼ cup lime juice*
- *3 tablespoons red wine vinegar*
- *3 tablespoons orange marmalade*
- *salt and freshly ground pepper to taste*
- *croutons (preferably homemade)*
- *⅓ cup halved pecans*
- *3 ounces bleu cheese, crumbled*

- Combine lettuce, kiwi fruits, oranges, and onion.
- Combine olive oil, lime juice, vinegar, and marmalade. Mix well.
- Toss salad with dressing just before serving.
- Top with croutons, nuts, and bleu cheese.

# *Spinach Salad with Hot Bacon Dressing*

*This warm, fragrant dressing gives spinach salad a new twist.*

- 3 *chicken-flavored bouillon cubes*
- 3 *cups water*
- 1 *cup sugar*
- ¾ *cup vinegar*
- ¼ *teaspoon salt*
- ¼ *pound bacon (7-8 strips)*
- ½ *cup chopped onion*
- ½ *cup flour*
- *freshly ground pepper to taste*
- 2 *bunches fresh spinach, washed, dried, and stems removed*

- Combine bouillon, water, sugar, vinegar, and salt in a saucepan and bring to a boil. Reduce heat and simmer.
- Dice bacon and fry. Remove bacon from pan. Add onion to drippings; fry until soft. When onion is soft, add flour to make a roux. When flour is bubbling, add water mixture, mixing with a whisk to blend. Serve hot over fresh spinach. Season with freshly ground pepper.

*If homemade chicken stock is available, substitute that for water and bouillon cubes.*

# *Mai Sun Salad*

*The perfect accompaniment to stir-fry meals*

1 *head lettuce (butter, red leaf, bibb, or romaine)*
*rice sticks (deep fried in hot oil until crisp)*
6 *scallions, sliced (including tops)*
1 *cup toasted sliced almonds*
½ *cup sesame seeds*
*homemade bacon bits*
*Mandarin orange sections, as desired*
4 *tablespoons sugar*
2-3 *teaspoons salt*
½ *teaspoon pepper*
4 *tablespoons red wine vinegar*
½ *cup vegetable oil*

- Combine lettuce, rice sticks, scallions, almonds, sesame seeds, bacon bits, and orange sections.
- Combine sugar, salt, pepper, vinegar, and vegetable oil. Mix well. Toss salad with dressing just before serving.

# *Chinese Cucumber Salad*

*Cool and refreshing!*

2 *large cucumbers, peeled*
½ *teaspoon salt*
1 *teaspoon sugar*
1 *tablespoon soy sauce*
1 *tablespoon wine vinegar*
1 *tablespoon sesame oil*

- Halve cucumbers lengthwise. Scrape out seeds and discard. Slice cucumbers.
- Mix together salt, sugar, soy sauce, vinegar, and oil. Add to cucumbers and toss. Chill.

## *Tomato and Mozzarella with Fresh Basil*

*Red, ripe, luscious tomatoes make this combination one of our favorites.*

- 2 *large red, ripe tomatoes, sliced*
- 8 *ounces fresh mozzarella cheese, sliced*
- 1 *medium red onion, thinly sliced (optional)*
- 4-5 *leaves fresh basil, cut into thin strips*
- 2 *tablespoons lemon juice or red wine vinegar*
- 1/3 *cup olive oil*

- Alternate slices of tomato, cheese and onion (if desired) on a serving platter. Sprinkle with snipped basil. Drizzle with lemon juice and olive oil.

## *Crunchy Broccoli Salad*

*A crisp addition to your picnic fare*

- 1 *bunch broccoli flowerets, blanched*
- 1/2 *red onion, chopped*
- 1/2 *cup sugar*
- 2 *tablespoons raspberry vinegar*
- 1/2 *cup mayonnaise*
- 1/2 *cup sour cream*
- 1/2 *cup chopped pecans*
- 8 *slices of bacon, crisply fried*

- Marinate broccoli and onion for 30 minutes in vinegar and sugar. Drain.
- Mix broccoli and onion with mayonnaise and sour cream. Add bacon and pecans.

*This recipe can also be prepared with cauliflower.*

## *Classic Coleslaw*

*This is the first of three great ways to serve coleslaw — from family favorites to company classics.*

- *1 head cabbage (2 to 3 pounds), cored and shredded*
- *2 carrots, peeled and shredded*
- *1 cup mayonnaise*
- *1 cup sour cream*
- *2 tablespoons Dijon mustard*
- *½ teaspoon salt*
- *½ teaspoon pepper*
- *¼ teaspoon bottled hot pepper sauce*

- Place cabbage in a large bowl of cold water. Let stand 1 hour to crisp. Drain in colander. Blot dry with paper towels.
- Stir together mayonnaise, sour cream, mustard, salt, pepper, and hot pepper sauce in a small bowl until well blended.
- Combine cabbage, carrots, and dressing in a large bowl. Toss until mixed well.

## *Avocado Slaw*

*Smooth!*

- *2 medium avocados, peeled and mashed*
- *2 tablespoons plus 1 teaspoon lemon juice*
- *4 cups (or more) shredded cabbage*
- *⅔ cup sliced scallions*
- *1 large sweet red pepper, roasted, seeded, peeled, and diced*
- *6 tablespoons mayonnaise*
- *1 teaspoon sugar*
- *1 tablespoon balsamic vinegar*
- *¾ teaspoon salt*
- *¼ teaspoon bottled hot pepper sauce*
- *1 teaspoon Worcestershire sauce*

- Mix avocado and lemon juice. Stir in cabbage and scallions. Add red pepper.
- Mix dressing by whisking together all remaining ingredients. Stir into cabbage mixture. Cover and refrigerate.

# *Oriental Cabbage Slaw*

*Intriguing!*

- *2/3 cup packed cilantro leaves*
- *1/4 cup rice wine vinegar*
- *1 1/2 teaspoons Dijon mustard*
- *1/2 teaspoon sugar*
- *1/2 teaspoon coriander*
- *1/4 teaspoon salt*
- *1/8 teaspoon cayenne pepper*
- *1/2 cup vegetable or peanut oil*
- *3 ounces snow peas, trimmed and cut diagonally into 1/2-inch pieces*
- *1/2 pound Chinese cabbage, shredded lengthwise*
- *1 sweet red pepper, cored, seeded, and julienned*
- *1 carrot, peeled and shredded*

- Combine first seven ingredients. Process in a blender until cilantro is finely chopped. Add oil. Whirl until well blended. Transfer to a large mixing bowl.

- Blanch snow peas in a pot of boiling salted water until crisp-tender and bright green, about 15 seconds. Drain; rinse under cold water; drain again. Dry well and add to bowl of dressing. Add cabbage, sweet red pepper, and carrot; toss to combine. Refrigerate 2 hours before serving.

# *Bavarian Potato Salad*

*A sure hit with the men in your life*

- 3-4 *slices bacon, cut into small pieces*
- 1 *small onion, chopped*
- 2 *tablespoons water*
- 3 *tablespoons sugar*
- ¼ *cup vinegar*
- 1 *tablespoon flour*
- 4 *cups sliced cooked potato*
- 2 *tablespoons chopped fresh parsley*
- *salt and pepper to taste*

- In a large pot, cook bacon until browned. Add onion and cook until translucent. Add water, sugar, and vinegar. Add flour to thicken. Allow to boil 1 to 2 minutes. Add potato and parsley. Heat thoroughly before serving. Salt and pepper to taste.

# *Country Inn Potato Salad*

*A great addition to the family reunion table*

- 5 *pounds red potatoes*
- 1 *pound bacon, diced*
- ¼ *cup Dijon mustard*
- 2 *tablespoons lemon juice*
- 1 *teaspoon each salt, white pepper, and black pepper*
- 1 *tablespoon basil*
- 2 *tablespoons chopped fresh parsley*
- 1 *medium onion, diced*
- 2 *cups mayonnaise*

- Boil potatoes until tender. Slice, leaving skins on. Set aside to cool.
- Sauté bacon until crisp. Combine with potatoes.
- Add remaining ingredients, except mayonnaise, and toss gently. Add mayonnaise to desired consistency. Chill salad for at least two hours before serving.

# *Wild Rice Salad*

*Salad with a nutty taste*

- 1 *cup wild rice*
- 4 *cups beef bouillon, undiluted*
- 2 *cups broccoli flowerets*
- 4 *celery stalks, cut diagonally and thinly sliced*
- 8 *scallions, sliced*
- ½ *cup toasted slivered almonds*

## *Dressing*

- 4 *tablespoons red wine vinegar*
- 2 *tablespoons soy sauce*
- 2 *tablespoons sugar*
- ½ *cup vegetable oil*
- 4 *teaspoons sesame oil*

- Place rice in a saucepan. Cover with water to about 1 inch above rice. Bring to a boil. Drain rice; add bouillon. Simmer, covered, until all liquid is absorbed, about 45 minutes.
- Blanch broccoli flowerets; drain. Mix broccoli with celery, scallions, and almonds.
- Combine dressing ingredients; add to rice. Toss while still warm. Combine with other ingredients. Mix well.
- Refrigerate or serve warm.

# *Cold Noodles with Sesame Sauce*

*This authentic recipe features several unusual ingredients. The flavorful result will more than justify your trip to the Oriental market.*

*3 tablespoons sesame oil*
*5 tablespoons soy sauce, divided*
*3 tablespoons red wine vinegar, divided*
*1 tablespoon plus 1½ teaspoons sugar, divided*
*3 tablespoons sesame paste*
*3 tablespoons dry sherry*
*1 tablespoon hot oil*
*1 teaspoon hoisin sauce*
*1½ teaspoons minced fresh ginger root*
*¾ pound capellini*
*½ medium cucumber, julienned*
*3 scallions, thinly sliced*

- In a small bowl, combine sesame oil, 3 tablespoons soy sauce, 2 tablespoons vinegar, and 1 tablespoon sugar. In a second small bowl, combine the remaining 2 tablespoons soy sauce, 1 tablespoon vinegar, and 1½ teaspoons sugar with the sesame paste, sherry, hot oil, hoisin sauce, and ginger. Stir until blended.

- Cook capellini; drain. Run under cold water and drain again very well.

- In a large bowl, toss capellini with sesame oil and soy mixture. Add sesame paste sauce. Toss. Sprinkle with cucumber and sliced scallions.

# *Tortellini-Broccoli Salad*

*Beautiful colors and fresh taste*

- *1 (16 ounce) package cheese tortellini or 1 (7 ounce) package each white and green pasta*
- *flowerets from 1 bunch of broccoli, chopped*
- *3-4 carrots, julienned*
- *½ cup finely chopped fresh parsley*
- *3 scallions, chopped*
- *1 teaspoon basil*
- *½ teaspoon garlic powder*
- *¾ cup Italian dressing (preferably homemade)*
- *cherry tomatoes, halved*
- *sliced olives*

- Cook tortellini. Drain; rinse with cold water.
- In a large bowl, combine all ingredients except tomatoes. Cover and refrigerate.
- Add tomatoes just before serving; mix well.

## *Lemonade Cream Mold*

*Smooth and soothing on a hot day...and absolutely elegant*

- *2 (3 ounce) packages lemon-flavored gelatin mix*
- *1 cup sugar*
- *¼ teaspoon salt*
- *2 cups boiling water*
- *1 (12 ounce) can frozen lemonade concentrate*
- *1 cup heavy cream, whipped*
- *fresh fruit in season*

- Combine gelatin mix, sugar, and salt in a bowl. Add boiling water; stir until dissolved. Stir in lemonade concentrate. Chill until mixture has a jelly-like consistency. Fold whipped cream into lemon mixture. Pour into an 8-cup ring mold. Chill.
- Unmold and fill with fresh fruit. (Melon balls, strawberries, sliced kiwi fruits, and blueberries are an excellent choice.)

## *Strawberry Pretzel Salad*

*Yes, pretzels!*

- *2½ cups crushed pretzels*
- *1 cup butter, melted*
- *3 tablespoons sugar*
- *8 ounces cream cheese, softened*
- *1 cup sugar*
- *1 cup heavy cream*
- *2 (3 ounce) packages strawberry-flavored gelatin mix*
- *2 cups hot water*
- *1 cup cold water*
- *1 quart sliced strawberries (fresh or frozen)*

- Mix crushed pretzels, butter, and sugar together. Pat into a 9x13-inch pan. Bake in a 400° oven for 10 minutes. Cool completely.
- Beat cream cheese and sugar together. Whip heavy cream until thick; fold into cream cheese mixture. Spread over pretzel crust. Put in refrigerator to set.
- Dissolve gelatin mix with 2 cups hot water. Add 1 cup cold water when slightly thickened. Stir in sliced strawberries. Pour over cream cheese layer. Refrigerate overnight.

# *Cran-Raspberry Ring*

*It doesn't have to be Thanksgiving to enjoy the refreshing taste of cranberries.*

- *1 (3 ounce) package raspberry-flavored gelatin mix*
- *1 (3 ounce) package lemon-flavored gelatin mix*
- *1¼ cups boiling water*
- *1 (10 ounce) package frozen unsweetened raspberries*
- *1 (12 ounce) bag fresh cranberries, washed and cleaned*
- *1 medium orange with peel, seeded and cut into 8 pieces*
- *1 cup lemon-lime soda*
- *lettuce*

- Finely chop cranberries in a food processor. Add orange slices and process until finely chopped. Set aside.
- Dissolve raspberry and lemon gelatin mixes in boiling water. Stir in frozen raspberries, breaking up large pieces with a fork. Stir in cranberry-orange mixture. Slowly pour in lemon-lime soda, stirring gently to combine all ingredients.
- Pour into a 6 or 6½-cup ring mold. Chill until firm. Unmold on lettuce-lined platter.

*This is a tangy alternative to the usual sweet cranberry sauce. It cleanses the palate, and is great with pork and poultry.*

# *Lemon Ginger Chicken Salad*

*This makes a lovely luncheon entrée; accompany it with a roll and a light dessert.*

*1/2 cup mayonnaise*
*1/4 cup sour cream*
*1 tablespoon sugar*
*1/2 teaspoon lemon zest*
*1 tablespoon lemon juice*
*1/4 teaspoon salt*
*1/2 teaspoon ginger*
*2 1/2 cups cooked, diced chicken*
*1 cup seedless green grapes*
*1 cup sliced celery*
*toasted, slivered almonds*
*fresh strawberries for garnish*

- Stir together first 7 ingredients. Add chicken, grapes, and celery, tossing to coat well. Cover and chill at least 2 to 3 hours.
- Serve in cantaloupe halves or on a bed of lettuce, topped with toasted, slivered almonds and garnished with fresh strawberries.

# *Grilled Chicken Toss*

*For a '90's palate, grill the chicken and hold the mayo!*

- *4 tablespoons vegetable oil, divided*
- *4 tablespoons fresh lime juice, divided*
- *1 teaspoon salt, divided*
- *1/4 teaspoon freshly ground pepper*
- *4 boneless, skinless chicken breasts*
- *1/8 teaspoon red pepper flakes*
- *1/8 teaspoon grated lime peel*
- *2 nectarines, thinly sliced*
- *2 plums, thinly sliced*
- *2 scallions, minced*
- *2 teaspoons grated fresh ginger root*
- *3 cups packed spinach leaves*
- *2 cups watercress*
- *julienned lime peel for garnish*

- Combine 1 tablespoon oil, 1 tablespoon lime juice, ½ teaspoon salt, and pepper in a shallow bowl. Add chicken; turn to coat. Refrigerate.
- Meanwhile, whisk remaining 3 tablespoons oil, 1 tablespoon lime juice, remaining ½ teaspoon salt, pepper flakes, and lime peel in a bowl. Toss fruit, scallions, remaining 2 tablespoons lime juice, and ginger together in another bowl.
- Preheat grill or broiler. Grill chicken 4 inches from heat source, 4 minutes per side. Slice chicken into ½-inch strips.
- Toss greens with lime dressing; place on platter. Top with chicken and spoon on fruit. Garnish with lime.

# *Pears à la Chicken Salad*

*Full-bodied and fruity*

- *1 (29 ounce) can pear halves*
- *½ cup sautérne wine*
- *2 cups cooked, diced chicken*
- *½ cup diced celery*
- *1 (11 ounce) can Mandarin orange sections*
- *1 cup seedless grapes*
- *¼ cup toasted slivered almonds or walnuts*
- *½ cup mayonnaise*
- *2 tablespoons lemon juice*
- *2 tablespoons soy sauce*
- *¼ teaspoon curry powder (optional)*

- Drain pear halves, reserving ½ cup syrup. Add wine to syrup and pour over pears. Refrigerate.
- Combine chicken, celery, oranges, grapes, and nuts. In a separate bowl, combine mayonnaise, lemon juice, soy sauce, and curry powder.
- Add mayonnaise mixture to chicken mixture and toss. Drain pears, place on a plate, and fill with chicken salad.

*Use your leftover turkey as an alternative to chicken.*

# *Oriental Chicken Salad*

*An innovative mix of ingredients*

- *8 ounces thin spaghetti*
- *2 large carrots, peeled*
- *2 tablespoons sesame seeds*
- *1/2 cup soy sauce*
- *1/3 cup vegetable oil*
- *1 tablespoon sugar*
- *1/2 tablespoon minced fresh ginger root (or 1 teaspoon ground)*
- *1 tablespoon white vinegar*
- *2 tablespoons creamy peanut butter*
- *1/4 teaspoon red pepper flakes*
- *2 whole boneless chicken breasts, cooked*
- *1/2 cup sliced scallions*

- Cook spaghetti. Meanwhile, cut carrots into strips. Add carrots to spaghetti during last 5 minutes of cooking. When both spaghetti and carrots are tender, drain. Rinse with cold water and return to pan.

- In a small saucepan, heat sesame seeds until golden brown. Remove from heat. Stir in soy sauce, oil, sugar, ginger, vinegar, peanut butter, and red pepper.

- Toss spaghetti and carrots with sauce. Cut chicken into strips and add with scallions to spaghetti.

*Best served warm or at room temperature.*

# *Salade Niçoise*

*Be creative in your presentation of this arranged salad.*

- *2 pounds green beans, cooked crisp-tender*
- *2 green peppers, sliced into rings*
- *1 pound cherry tomatoes*
- *5 medium red potatoes, cooked, peeled, and sliced*
- *3 (7 ounce) cans tuna, drained*
- *1 (2 ounce) can flat anchovy fillets*
- *10 stuffed green olives*
- *10 black olives*
- *1 large red onion, sliced*
- *6 hard boiled eggs, quartered*
- *2 tablespoons chopped fresh basil (or 1 teaspoon dried)*
- *1/3 cup minced fresh parsley*
- *1/4 cup chopped scallions*

## *Dressing*

- *2 teaspoons Dijon mustard*
- *2 tablespoons wine vinegar*
- *1 1/2 teaspoons salt*
- *1-2 cloves garlic*
- *6 tablespoons vegetable oil*
- *6 tablespoons olive oil*
- *freshly ground pepper*
- *1 teaspoon chopped fresh thyme (or 1/2 teaspoon dried)*

- Combine dressing ingredients in a bowl. Blend well.
- Arrange first 10 salad ingredients attractively on a large platter. Sprinkle with chopped herbs. Drizzle with dressing just before serving.

# *Fresh Pasta and Lobster Salad*

*An impressive gourmet dish*

- *8 ounces spirals or other fancy pasta, cooked*
- *¼ cup very thinly sliced shallots*
- *1 tablespoon red wine vinegar*
- *3 tablespoons olive oil*
- *2 cloves garlic, lightly crushed*
- *¼ teaspoon salt*
- *freshly ground pepper*
- *1 lobster (about 1½ pounds), cooked, meat removed*
- *2 tablespoons lemon juice*
- *½ pound snow peas, stems and strings removed, sliced in half diagonally*
- *1 tablespoon chopped fresh basil*

- Place half of the shallots in a bowl with vinegar and let stand for five minutes. Whisk in 2 tablespoons oil. Stir in garlic, ⅛ teaspoon salt, and pepper. Set aside.
- Cut lobster into ½-inch pieces and set aside in a bowl.
- Pour remaining tablespoon of oil into a large, heavy-bottomed skillet over medium-high heat. Add snow peas, remaining 2 tablespoons shallots, and ⅛ teaspoon of salt. Cook, stirring constantly, until snow peas turn bright green (about 90 seconds). Empty contents of skillet into bowl with lobster.
- Remove and discard garlic from vinaigrette. Combine vinaigrette with pasta. Add lobster mixture, basil, remaining tablespoon of lemon juice, and pepper. Toss well.

*Shrimp can be substituted for lobster.*

# *Pizza Salad*

*Salad and pizza-lovers—now, you can have the best of both worlds.*

- 1 *bag pizza dough*
- 1/4 *cup olive oil*
- 1/2 *teaspoon basil*
- 1/8-1/4 *teaspoon crushed red pepper flakes*
- 8 *ounces mozzarella cheese, cut into 1/2-inch cubes*
- 1/4 *cup sliced, pitted black olives*
- 1 *(6 ounce) jar marinated artichoke hearts, undrained*
- 3 *cups broccoli flowerets and tender stems*
- 1/2 *cup green beans, cut into 1-inch lengths*
- 2 *tablespoons tarragon vinegar*
- 2 *teaspoons finely chopped shallots or onion*
- 1 *small sweet yellow or red pepper, halved, seeded and cut into 1/4-inch wide strips*
- 3 *radishes, thinly sliced*
- 12-18 *slices salami, cut into wedges*
- 2 *cups shredded crisp lettuce (romaine, escarole, or iceberg)*
- 3 *medium tomatoes, each cut into about 8 wedges*
- *alfalfa sprouts for garnish*
- *chopped fresh parsley for garnish*

- Prepare pizza dough. Bake at 400° for 20 to 25 minutes, or as directed on package.
- Combine oil, basil, pepper flakes, cheese, olives, and undrained artichoke hearts in a bowl; stir to mix. Marinate in refrigerator, stirring once or twice, for 2 to 3 hours.
- Meanwhile, cook broccoli and green beans in a large saucepan of boiling water for 1 minute. Drain; plunge into ice water to stop cooking. Drain; refrigerate.
- About 30 minutes before serving, combine broccoli, green beans, vinegar, shallots, pepper, radishes, and salami to marinated cheese mixture. Toss.
- Spread lettuce over pizza crust. Arrange tomato wedges around outside edge, overlapping rim slightly. With a slotted spoon, spoon salad into center. Drizzle any remaining dressing from bowl over tomatoes. Garnish with alfalfa sprouts and sprinkle with parsley. To serve, cut into wedges.

# *Extra-Ordinary Taco Salad*

*Your family will say, "Olé."*

- *3/4 pound lean ground beef*
- *1 large yellow onion, chopped*
- *1 small sweet green pepper, cored, seeded, and chopped*
- *2 cloves garlic, minced*
- *1 1/2 teaspoons chili powder*
- *1 (16 ounce) can tomatoes, chopped, with 1/3 cup juice reserved*
- *2 tablespoons cider vinegar*
- *2 teaspoons tomato paste*
- *1/2 teaspoon ginger*
- *1/2 teaspoon thyme*
- *1/4 teaspoon pepper*
- *1 small head iceberg lettuce, trimmed, cored, and shredded*
- *1/2 cup plain low-fat yogurt, whisked until creamy*
- *2 scallions, thinly sliced*
- *3 medium radishes, chopped*
- *2 tablespoons shredded cheddar cheese*

- Heat a heavy 10-inch skillet over moderate heat for 30 seconds. Add ground beef and cook, stirring, until no longer pink (3 to 4 minutes). Push meat to one side of skillet.
- Add onion and green pepper; cook, stirring, about 5 minutes. Add garlic and chili powder; cook and stir 2 minutes more. Add tomatoes, vinegar, tomato paste, ginger, thyme, and pepper. Simmer, uncovered, for 30 minutes, stirring occasionally.
- To serve, make a bed of lettuce and mound meat mixture on top. Spoon yogurt into center. Top with scallions, radishes, and cheese.

## *Sweet and Sour Salad Dressing*

*Here is the first of three traditional dressings. After you've tried homemade, you'll never want bottled dressing again!*

- ½ *cup sugar*
- 1 *teaspoon each dry mustard, paprika, and salt*
- 2 *tablespoons chopped onion*
- ½ *cup cider vinegar*
- 2 *tablespoons lemon juice*
- ½ *cup honey*
- 1 *cup peanut oil*

• Combine all ingredients. Mix well. Keep refrigerated.

*This dressing complements a salad made with crisply fried bacon, Mandarin orange sections, red onion rings, and pecans.*

## *Honey Garlic Dressing*

*Sweet!*

- 1 *cup honey*
- ½ *cup oil*
- 5 *tablespoons vinegar (tarragon or wine)*
- 1 *clove garlic, minced*
- 1 *tablespoon celery seed*
- *salt to taste*

• Combine all ingredients. Mix well. Keep refrigerated.

## *French Dressing*

*Tangy!*

- 1 *cup sugar*
- *salt to taste*
- ½ *cup vinegar*
- 1 *cup ketchup*
- *juice of 2 lemons*
- 1½ *cups vegetable oil*
- 1 *clove garlic*

• Place first 5 ingredients in a bowl. Beat with rotary beater until blended. Add oil slowly; continue beating until well blended. Add garlic clove. Let stand for 1 hour, then remove garlic clove.

*For a delicious variation, try adding crumbled bleu cheese.*

# BREADS & BRUNCH

# BREADS & BRUNCH



*Breads*



*Brunch*

## Grandma's Cinnamon Banana Bread

*When my grandmother baked, all the children in the neighborhood came by for samples of her bread.*

- *½ cup butter*
- *1 cup sugar*
- *2 eggs*
- *3 large, ripe bananas, mashed*
- *2 cups flour*
- *1 teaspoon baking soda*
- *½ teaspoon salt*
- *1 cup chopped walnuts (optional)*
- *1 teaspoon butter, melted cinnamon-sugar mixture*

*Makes 1 loaf*

- Cream butter and sugar. Beat in eggs, one at a time. Mix in mashed bananas.
- Sift dry ingredients together; stir into banana mixture. Add nuts.
- Pour into a greased 9x5x3-inch loaf pan. Bake at 350° for 1 hour, or until a toothpick inserted into loaf comes out clean.
- While cake is still warm, pour melted butter over top and sprinkle with a mixture of cinnamon and sugar.

*Bread can be frozen.*

## Chocolate Zucchini Bread

*The perfect combination*

- *3 eggs*
- *2 cups sugar*
- *2 teaspoons vanilla*
- *2 cups flour*
- *¾ cup cocoa*
- *1 teaspoon baking soda*
- *1 teaspoon salt*
- *½ teaspoon baking powder*
- *2 cups shredded zucchini*
- *¾ cup vegetable oil*
- *1 cup semi-sweet chocolate chips*

- Beat eggs, sugar, and vanilla. Mix in dry ingredients. Add zucchini. Stir to combine.
- Add oil and beat until smooth. Stir in chocolate chips.
- Pour into 2 greased 9x5x13-inch loaf pans and bake at 325° for 1 hour.

# *Fresh Strawberry Bread*

*When sprinkled with powdered sugar, this makes a delicious breakfast treat.*

- *1 cup flour*
- *1/2 cup sugar*
- *1 1/2 teaspoons cinnamon*
- *1/2 teaspoon salt*
- *1/2 teaspoon baking soda*
- *2 eggs, beaten*
- *3/4 cup vegetable oil*
- *1 pint fresh strawberries, sliced*
- *3/4 cup chopped walnuts or pecans*

- Mix dry ingredients. Add liquid ingredients. Add strawberries and nuts. Mix well and pour into a greased 9x5x3-inch loaf pan.
- Bake at 350° for 1 hour.

# *Citrus Bread*

*Richer than a bread—but not as sweet as a cake*

- *1/2 cup shortening*
- *1 cup sugar*
- *1/2 cup milk*
- *2 eggs*
- *1 1/2 cups flour*
- *1 teaspoon baking powder*
- *1 teaspoon salt*
- *zest from 1 lemon*
- *1/2 cup chopped walnuts or pecans*
- *juice of one lemon mixed with 2 tablespoons sugar*

- Mix together shortening, sugar, and milk. Beat in eggs one at a time.
- Mix in flour, baking powder, salt, lemon zest, and nuts.
- Pour into a greased 9x5x3-inch loaf pan. Bake at 350° for 1 hour.
- While bread is still warm, spread lemon juice and sugar mixture over the loaf.

*For a change of pace, substitute orange or lime wherever lemon is used.*

## *Toasted Coconut Bread*

*The coconut adds a surprise (almost secret) ingredient.*

- *1 cup toasted shredded coconut*
- *2 cups unbleached flour*
- *1 tablespoon baking powder*
- *½ teaspoon salt*
- *¾ cup sugar*
- *1 cup milk*
- *1 egg, well beaten*
- *¼ cup vegetable oil*
- *1 teaspoon vanilla*

*Makes 1 loaf*

- Combine dry ingredients. In a separate bowl, mix milk, egg, oil, and vanilla together. Add to dry ingredients. Stir until blended.
- Pour into a greased and floured 9x5x3-inch loaf pan. Bake at 350° for 1 hour.

## *Apricot Bread*

*Flavorful in any season.*

- *3 cups sifted flour*
- *1½ teaspoons baking soda*
- *½ teaspoon salt*
- *2 cups sugar*
- *1½ cups vegetable oil*
- *4 large eggs*
- *1 teaspoon vanilla*
- *1 (5 ounce) can evaporated milk*
- *1 cup apricot butter*
- *½ cup chopped nuts*

### *Apricot Butter*

- *1 cup finely chopped apricots, soaked overnight in water*
- *1 cup sugar*

*Makes 2 loaves*

- Mix together flour, baking soda, and salt. Add sugar, oil, eggs, vanilla, and evaporated milk. Mix thoroughly. Add apricot butter and nuts; blend.
- Pour into 2 greased and floured 9x5x3-inch loaf pans and bake at 350° for 1 hour and 15 minutes.
- *Apricot Butter* — Soak apricots overnight in water to cover. Add sugar and simmer 10 minutes, or until soft. Cool completely.

# *Carrot Zucchini Muffins*

*This is a favorite recipe from Captain Kangaroo. We're wondering, does Bunny Rabbit deliver the carrots?*

- *3 tablespoons shortening*
- *1/2 cup firmly packed brown sugar*
- *2 egg whites, lightly beaten*
- *2/3 cup skim milk*
- *1 3/4 cups quick or old-fashioned oats, uncooked*
- *1 cup flour*
- *1 tablespoon baking powder*
- *1/4 teaspoon nutmeg*
- *1 cup shredded carrot*
- *1/2 cup shredded zucchini*

## *Topping*

- *1/4 cup quick or old-fashioned oats, uncooked*
- *1 tablespoon chopped almonds*
- *1 tablespoon shortening, melted*

*Makes 1 dozen muffins*

- Combine shortening and brown sugar in a large bowl. Beat at medium speed with an electric mixer or stir with a fork until well blended. Gradually stir in egg whites and milk. Combine oats, flour, baking powder, and nutmeg. Stir into liquid ingredients. Add carrots and zucchini. Stir until just blended. Fill foil or paper-lined muffin cups.
- To prepare topping, combine oats, nuts, and shortening. Sprinkle over each muffin. Press into batter lightly. Bake at 400° for 20 to 25 minutes, or until golden brown. Serve warm.

## *Healthy Start Bran Muffins*

*A great way to have breakfast on the run*

- 2 *cups boiling water*
- 1 *cup raisins*
- 2 *cups all-bran cereal*
- 2½ *cups sugar*
- 1¼ *cups vegetable oil*
- 4 *eggs*
- 1 *quart buttermilk*
- 4 *cups bran buds*
- 6 *cups flour*
- 5 *teaspoons baking soda*
- 2 *teaspoons baking powder*
- 2 *teaspoons salt*

*Makes 3 dozen*

- Combine boiling water, all-bran cereal, and raisins. Allow to cool. Cream together sugar, oil, eggs, buttermilk, and bran buds. Add to raisin and bran mixture. Mix well.
- Sift together flour, baking soda, baking powder, and salt; add to other ingredients. Fill greased or paper-lined muffin cups. Bake at 375° for 25 minutes.

*This mixture can be refrigerated 4 weeks.*

## *Blueberry Corn Muffins*

*A delicious way to enjoy the fruits of summer...healthy, too*

- 1 *cup flour*
- 1 *cup corn meal*
- ⅔ *cup sugar*
- 1 *tablespoon baking powder*
- ½ *teaspoon salt*
- ¼ *cup vegetable oil*
- 1 *egg*
- 1 *cup skim milk*
- 1 *cup blueberries*

*Makes 1 dozen*

- Combine flour, corn meal, sugar, baking powder, and salt in a large bowl. Add oil, egg, and skim milk, stirring until just moist. Gently stir in blueberries. Fill greased or paper-lined muffin cups.
- Bake at 400° for 20 minutes.

# *Pumpkin Apple Streusel Muffins*

*For your family gatherings around the breakfast table, when plain muffins just won't do*

- 2½ *cups flour*
- 2 *cups sugar*
- 1 *tablespoon pumpkin pie spice*
- 1 *teaspoon baking soda*
- ½ *teaspoon salt*
- 2 *eggs, lightly beaten*
- 1 *cup canned, cooked, pumpkin*
- ½ *cup vegetable oil*
- 2 *cups peeled and finely chopped apples*

## *Streusel Topping*

- 2 *tablespoons flour*
- ¼ *cup sugar*
- ½ *teaspoon cinnamon*
- 4 *teaspoons butter*

*Makes 1½ dozen muffins*

- Prepare topping by combining flour, sugar, and cinnamon in a small bowl. Cut in butter until mixture is crumbly. Set mixture aside.
- In a large bowl, combine flour, sugar, spice, baking soda, and salt. Set aside.
- In a medium bowl, combine eggs, pumpkin, and oil. Add liquid ingredients to dry ingredients; stir just until moistened. Stir in apples.
- Fill greased or paper-lined muffin cups. Sprinkle streusel topping over batter.
- Bake at 350° for 35 to 40 minutes.

# *Sour Cream Coffee Cake*

*This has always been a favorite recipe for slumber parties. It is easy enough to make at midnight...delicious to eat in the early hours...and then again at breakfast time.*

- *2 cups flour*
- *1 teaspoon baking powder*
- *1 teaspoon baking soda*
- *½ cup butter*
- *1 cup sugar*
- *2 eggs*
- *1 teaspoon vanilla*
- *1 cup sour cream*

## *Filling*

- *¼ cup firmly packed brown sugar*
- *1 teaspoon cinnamon*
- *½ cup chopped walnuts (optional)*

- Combine flour, baking powder, and baking soda.
- Cream butter and sugar. Add eggs and vanilla. Alternately mix in flour and sour cream.
- Combine filling ingredients in a separate bowl.
- Pour half the batter into a greased tube pan. Sprinkle half the filling over it. Pour in remaining batter. Sprinkle remaining filling on top.
- Bake at 375° for 55 minutes.

# *Italian Bread*

*When you need fresh-from-the-oven bread to go with that perfect pasta dish*

*1 tablespoon sugar*
*2 teaspoons salt*
*2 packages dry yeast*
*5 cups flour*
*1 tablespoon butter*
*water*
*vegetable oil*
*1 egg white*

- Combine sugar, salt, yeast, and 2 cups flour. Melt butter in 1¾ cups hot water. Do not allow to boil.

- Beat liquid into dry ingredients. Beat in an additional ½ cup flour. Stir in 1¾ cups flour until soft dough forms. Knead, adding flour as necessary.

- Cut dough into thirds. Let rest 20 minutes.

- Roll out each piece of dough. Roll up tightly. Pinch ends to seal. Place seam-side down on a paper-lined sheet. Brush loaves with oil. Refrigerate at least 2 hours, but not more than 2 days.

- Remove loaves from refrigerator. Let stand 10 minutes. Cut 3 or 4 slashes in top of each loaf. Bake at 400° for 20 minutes.

- Beat egg white in 1 tablespoon water. Remove loaves from oven. Brush with egg white. Bake an additional 5 minutes.

## *New York Cheddar Cheese Bread*

*All you need is soup to make this hearty bread a delectable meal on a winter's night.*

- *2 cups sifted flour*
- *2 teaspoons baking powder*
- *1 tablespoon sugar*
- *½ teaspoon salt*
- *¼ cup butter*
- *1 cup grated sharp cheddar cheese*
- *1 tablespoon grated onion*
- *1½ teaspoons dill*
- *¾ cup milk*
- *1 egg, lightly beaten*

*Makes 1 loaf*

- Sift flour with baking powder, sugar, and salt. Using 2 knives or a pastry blender, cut in butter until mixture resembles coarse crumbs. Stir in cheese, onion, and dill; mix well.
- Combine milk and egg; pour into flour mixture. Stir until moistened.
- Turn into a greased 9x5x3-inch loaf pan. Bake at 350° for 40 to 50 minutes, or until done.
- Let cool 10 minutes before removing from pan. Serve slightly warm.

## *Cottage Cheese and Dill Bread*

*Let this herbed bread, shared with us by skater Peggy Fleming Jenkins, grace your table just as she has graced the ice over the years.*

- *2 packages dry yeast*
- *2 teaspoons sugar*
- *½ cup warm water*
- *2 cups cottage cheese*
- *2 tablespoons minced dried onion flakes*
- *2 tablespoons dill*
- *1 teaspoon baking soda*
- *2 teaspoons salt*
- *2 tablespoons sugar*
- *2 eggs*
- *4-4½ cups flour*

*Makes 3 loaves*

- Combine yeast, sugar, and warm water. Set aside.
- Mix together cottage cheese, onion flakes, dill, baking soda, salt, and sugar. Add eggs and yeast mixture. Stir to combine. Add flour, ½ cup at a time. Knead.
- Allow dough to rise until it has doubled in size, approximately 1 to 1½ hours. Punch down and knead again. Divide dough into thirds.
- Bake in 3 greased 9x5x3-inch loaf pans at 350° for 30 minutes.

# *Oniony Dinner Rolls*

*You won't want to wait 'til dinner to taste one.*

- *2 cups warm water*
- *2 packages dry yeast*
- *1/3 cup sugar*
- *1 teaspoon salt*
- *2 tablespoons molasses (or cola soda)*
- *1 envelope onion soup mix*
- *1 egg, well beaten*
- *6 cups unsifted flour*
- *6 tablespoons shortening, melted*

*Makes 4 dozen rolls*

- Pour warm water into a large bowl. Sprinkle in yeast. Stir to dissolve.
- Add sugar, salt, molasses, and onion soup mix. Stir to combine.
- Add egg and 3 cups flour; beat well.
- Add shortening and remaining flour; beat well.
- On a lightly-floured board, knead bread until smooth (8 to 10 minutes). Cover and let rise in a warm place until doubled, about 45 minutes. Punch down. Shape into rolls. Cover and let rise until doubled, about 45 minutes.
- Bake at 400° for 15 to 20 minutes. Remove from oven and brush lightly with melted butter.

# *Heirloom Wheat Crescents*

*This recipe has been handed down from one generation to the next.*

*1½ cups boiling water*
*⅓ cup sugar*
*3 tablespoons butter*
*1⅓ cups shredded wheat crumbs*
*2 packages dry yeast*
*¼ cup warm water*
*1 egg*
*3¼-3½ cups flour*

*Makes 2 dozen rolls*

- Combine boiling water, sugar, butter, and shredded wheat. Stir until butter is melted; cool to lukewarm.

- Dissolve yeast in warm water. Add to shredded wheat mixture. Add egg and 2 cups flour; beat until smooth. Stir in remaining flour, mixing well to make a soft dough. Cover tightly with foil. Refrigerate at least 3 hours, but not more than 2 days.

- Grease 2 baking sheets. Remove dough from refrigerator; punch down. Divide dough in half. On a lightly-floured board, roll each half into a 13-inch circle; cut each into 12 pie-shaped wedges. Beginning at wide end, roll each wedge tightly; pressing ends to seal. Place on baking sheets; curve into crescent shapes. Cover with a dry towel. Let rise until doubled (1 hour).

- Bake at 375° for 18 to 20 minutes, or until lightly browned. Remove to rack. Serve warm.

*If preparing ahead of time, wrap in foil and refrigerate until serving time. Reheat in foil at 300° for 15 minutes.*

## *Soft Pretzels*

*These are a great alternative to cup cakes for your child's birthday celebration at school. Just shape the pretzels into the appropriate age!*

- *1 package dry yeast*
- *1½ cups warm water*
- *1 teaspoon salt*
- *1 tablespoon sugar*
- *4 cups flour*
- *1 large egg, beaten*
- *coarse salt*

- Dissolve yeast in warm water. Add salt and sugar. Blend in flour; knead dough until smooth.
- Cut dough into small pieces; roll into ropes. Twist ropes into desired pretzel shapes and place on foil-lined cookie sheets. Brush with egg and sprinkle with salt.
- Bake at 425° for 12 to 15 minutes, or until brown.

## *Spiral Breadsticks*

*Here's a great way to keep little hands busy while you prepare for guests. The children will glow with pride over the tasty outcome.*

- *8 refrigerated breadsticks*
- *2 teaspoons milk*
- *½ teaspoon sesame seeds, poppy seeds, paprika, or lemon-pepper seasoning*
- *16 (10- to 12-inch) wooden chopsticks or metal skewers*

- Unwind dough to form strips. Cut strips in half, lengthwise.
- Grease chopsticks or skewers. Roll one strip around each chopstick, stretching dough slightly and leaving ¼ inch of space between twists. Place on a greased baking sheet, tucking ends of dough under to secure.
- Brush rolls with milk; sprinkle with seasoning.
- Bake at 325° for 15 to 20 minutes, or until golden. Remove chopsticks before serving; serve warm.

# *Mom's Pancakes*

*Mom used to make big pancakes the size of a 9-inch frying pan. They were great, but you only ate "one" of hers.*

*2 cups flour*
*2 teaspoons sugar*
*2 teaspoons baking powder*
*2 tablespoons vegetable oil*
*1 egg*
*2 cups milk*
*1 tablespoon vanilla*

*Makes about 8 pancakes*

- Mix dry ingredients together, forming a well. Mix wet ingredients together and stir into flour mixture. Stir until wet, but a little lumpy.
- Drop by ⅓ cup measure onto a greased griddle and turn when "dry" on top. Griddle should be hot, but not too hot. Grease between pancakes.

# *Silver Dollar Pancakes*

*These tiny pancakes may trigger a pancake-eating contest at your family's table.*

*2 cups buttermilk*
*2 eggs*
*1½ cups flour*
*2 teaspoons baking powder*
*1 teaspoon baking soda*
*1 teaspoon salt*
*butter*

*Makes 20 pancakes*

- Beat buttermilk and eggs together with an electric mixer for about 2 minutes. Sift dry ingredients and blend into buttermilk mixture.
- Heat ½ tablespoon of butter in a non-stick frying pan until bubbly. When pan is ready, use a small gravy ladle to spoon out batter. Pancakes should be "silver dollar" size. When bubbles appear, flip pancake and continue cooking. Prepare in batches, keeping cooked pancakes warm on a plate in the oven.
- Serve with your favorite jam or syrup.

# *Thanksgiving Pancakes*

*Rich, moist, and luscious*

- *2 cups biscuit mix*
- *2 tablespoons light brown sugar*
- *2 teaspoons cinnamon*
- *1 teaspoon allspice*
- *1½ cups (12 ounce can) undiluted evaporated milk*
- *½ cup canned, cooked pumpkin*
- *2 tablespoons vegetable oil*
- *2 eggs*
- *1 teaspoon vanilla*

*Makes 16 pancakes*

- In a large mixing bowl, combine biscuit mix, sugar, cinnamon, and allspice. Add evaporated milk, pumpkin, oil, eggs, and vanilla; beat until smooth. Pour ¼ to ½ cup batter onto a heated and lightly-greased griddle.
- Cook until top surface is bubbly and edges are dry. Turn; cook until golden. Keep pancakes warm. Serve with syrup or honey.

# *Special Occasion Pancakes*

*Delicious, but don't let anyone in on the ingredients...*

- *1 cup cottage cheese*
- *6 eggs*
- *¾ cup flour*
- *¼ teaspoon salt*
- *¼ cup vegetable oil*
- *¼ cup milk*
- *½ teaspoon vanilla*

*Makes 1 dozen pancakes*

- Put all ingredients into a blender. Blend at high speed until well mixed.
- Cook on a greased, hot griddle.

## *Puffed Pancake with Strawberries*

*No-fuss breakfast with an elegant flair*

- *6 eggs*
- *1 cup milk*
- *1/4 cup orange juice*
- *1/2 cup sugar*
- *1 cup flour*
- *1/4 teaspoon salt*
- *1/4 cup butter*
- *1 pint strawberries, hulled and sliced*
- *confectioner's sugar*

- Mix eggs, milk, orange juice, sugar, flour, and salt in a blender. Melt butter in a 9-inch round glass pie plate in oven until sizzling. Do not allow butter to brown.
- Pour batter into baking dish. Bake at 350° in middle of oven until puffed and brown, about 20 minutes.
- Fill pancake with sliced strawberries. Sprinkle with confectioner's sugar.

## *Lemon Poppy Seed Waffles*

*A zingy start to your day*

- *2 eggs, lightly beaten*
- *2 cups packaged pancake mix*
- *2 1/2 (8 ounce) containers lemon yogurt*
- *1/4 cup vegetable oil*
- *2 tablespoons poppy seeds*
- *lemon zest*

*Makes 8 waffles*

- In a large mixing bowl, combine eggs, pancake mix, 2 containers yogurt, oil, and poppy seeds. Stir just until combined, but still slightly lumpy.
- Pour 1½ cups batter evenly onto bottom grid of a lightly-greased, hot waffle iron. Spread slightly. Close lid quickly; do not open during baking. Bake 4 to 5 minutes. Repeat with remaining batter.
- Serve immediately with remaining lemon yogurt and sprinkle with lemon zest.

# *Gingerbread Waffles*

*Spicy and special*

- 2 *cups gingersnap crumbs*
- 2 *cups flour*
- 1 *tablespoon plus 1 teaspoon baking powder*
- 2 *teaspoons cinnamon*
- 1 *teaspoon ginger*
- ¾ *teaspoon baking soda*
- ½ *teaspoon salt*
- 3 *eggs, separated*
- 1½ *cups buttermilk*
- ⅔ *cup butter, melted and cooled*
- ½ *cup honey*

*Makes 20 waffles*

- Combine first 7 ingredients in a large bowl; mix well. Set aside. Beat egg yolks in a small mixing bowl until thick and pale. Gradually add buttermilk, butter, and honey, beating constantly at medium speed until ingredients are well blended. Pour into dry ingredients; stir just until moistened. Set aside.
- Beat egg whites until stiff peaks form. Gently fold into batter. Spoon batter onto a preheated, lightly-oiled waffle iron. Cook until crisp.

# *French Toast with Brandied Lemon Butter*

*Fabulous at a New Year's Eve party, served just after midnight*

- 4 *eggs*
- 2 *tablespoons plus 1 teaspoon sugar*
- ½ *teaspoon salt*
- 1 *cup milk*
- ¼ *teaspoon vanilla*
- 12 *thick slices slightly stale bread*
- *butter*
- *confectioner's sugar*
- *lemon slices for garnish*

## *Brandied Lemon Butter*

- ½ *cup butter, clarified*
- 1 *cup sugar*
- *juice of 2 lemons*
- 4 *teaspoons grated lemon zest*
- 3 *ounces brandy or rum*

*Serves 6*

- In a shallow dish, beat eggs, sugar, salt, milk, and vanilla. Soak bread in mixture. Heat butter over medium-high heat and cook each slice until lightly browned on each side.
- Combine clarified butter and sugar in a saucepan over low heat. Stir until sugar dissolves. Add lemon zest, juice, and brandy. Stir until smooth.
- Pour brandied lemon butter over warm French toast. Sprinkle with confectioner's sugar. Garnish with lemon slices.

# *Beignets*

*These French doughnuts are the perfect choice when sipping your favorite coffee.*

*2¾-3¼ cups flour*
*1 package dry yeast*
*½ teaspoon nutmeg*
*1 cup milk*
*¼ cup sugar*
*2 tablespoons shortening*
*½ teaspoon salt*
*1 egg*
*shortening or vegetable oil for deep frying*
*confectioner's sugar*

*Makes 36*

- In a large mixing bowl, stir together 1½ cups flour, yeast, and nutmeg. In a saucepan, heat milk, sugar, shortening, and salt until warm (115 to 120°) and shortening has almost melted. Stir constantly. Add heated mixture to flour mixture. Add egg. Beat mixture on low speed until just combined. Beat 3 minutes on high speed.
- Using a spoon, stir in enough of the remaining flour to make a soft dough. Place dough in a greased bowl; turn once to grease the surface. Cover and refrigerate until well chilled.
- Turn dough out onto a lightly-floured surface. Cover; let rest 10 minutes. Roll into an 18x12-inch rectangle; cut into 3x2-inch rectangles. Cover; let rest 30 minutes (dough will not have doubled).
- Fry 2 or 3 dough rectangles at a time in deep hot fat (375°) about 1 minute, turning once. Drain on paper towels. Sprinkle with sifted confectioner's sugar.

# *Overnight Breakfast Casserole*

*A great start on a cold day*

- *1 (6 ounce) box dehydrated hash browns with onions*
- *5 eggs*
- *½ cup cottage cheese*
- *1 cup shredded cheddar cheese*
- *1 scallion, sliced*
- *freshly ground pepper to taste*
- *4 drops bottled hot pepper sauce*
- *6-9 slices cooked Canadian bacon, chopped*
- *paprika*

*Serves 6 to 8*

- *The night before* — Empty box of potatoes into a large bowl. Cover with 1 quart of hot tap water. Let stand 10 minutes. Drain in colander. Beat eggs. Stir in potatoes, cheeses, scallion, and seasonings. Turn into a buttered 10-inch round pie plate. Sprinkle bacon and paprika on top. Cover with plastic wrap and refrigerate.
- *The next day* — Place cold dish, uncovered, in a cold oven. Bake at 350° for 40 minutes, or until lightly browned.

*To serve after mixing, bake only 30 minutes.*

# *24 Hour Omelette*

*Great for a crowd*

- 1 *loaf day-old French bread, sliced*
- 6 *tablespoons butter, melted*
- ¾ *pound Swiss cheese*
- ½ *pound Monterey Jack cheese*
- 2 *pounds bulk sausage, browned*
- 16 *eggs*
- 3¼ *cups milk*
- ½ *cup dry white wine*
- 4 *large scallions, sliced*
- 1 *teaspoon dry mustard*
- ¼ *teaspoon pepper*
- ⅛ *teaspoon cayenne pepper*
- 1½ *cups sour cream*
- 1 *cup grated Parmesan cheese*

• Butter two 9x13-inch pans. Layer bread in both pans; sprinkle first with cheese, then with sausage. Beat together next 7 ingredients and pour over bread mixture. Cover and refrigerate overnight.

• Remove pans from refrigerator 30 minutes before baking. Bake at 325° for 1 hour. Remove from oven; spread with sour cream. Sprinkle Parmesan cheese on top; continue baking 10 more minutes.

## *Tomato Mozzarella Strata*

*Consider this when your kids want pizza for breakfast.*

- 12 *slices bread*
- *soft butter*
- 6 *slices salami*
- 8 *ounces mozzarella cheese, sliced*
- 2 *medium tomatoes, thinly sliced*
- 1/4 *cup finely chopped green peppers*
- 4 *eggs*
- 2 *cups milk*
- 1 *teaspoon basil*
- 1/2 *teaspoon salt*
- 1/4 *teaspoon oregano*
- 1/8 *teaspoon garlic powder*
- *tomato and green pepper slices for garnish*

- Trim crusts from bread; butter each slice. Place 6 slices buttered-side-up in a greased 12x7x2-inch baking dish.
- Layer salami, cheese, tomato, and green pepper on top of bread. Top with remaining slices of bread, buttered-side-up.
- Beat eggs in a bowl; add milk, basil, salt, oregano, and garlic powder. Spoon evenly over contents of baking dish. Cover and refrigerate at least 1 hour.
- Bake at 325° for 1 hour. Garnish, if desired, with thin slices of tomato and green pepper 10 minutes before end of baking.

## *Broccoli, Onion, and Mushroom Quiche*

*A golden classic*

- *1 (9-inch) unbaked pie shell*
- *1½ cups grated cheddar or Swiss cheese*
- *1 medium onion, chopped*
- *¼ pound fresh mushrooms, sliced*
- *2 tablespoons vegetable oil*
- *1 cup cooked broccoli*
- *3 eggs*
- *1 cup heavy cream*
- *3 tablespoons flour*
- *¼ teaspoon salt*

- Cover bottom of pie shell with shredded cheese.
- Sauté onion and mushrooms. Cover cheese with onion, mushrooms, and broccoli.
- Beat together eggs, cream, flour, and salt. Pour over vegetable layer.
- Bake at 375° for 40 to 45 minutes, or until top is golden brown and mixture is set.

## *Ricotta and Spinach Pie*

*Perfect for morning company*

- *1 (10 ounce) package frozen chopped spinach*
- *½ cup grated Parmesan cheese*
- *3 eggs*
- *2 pounds ricotta cheese*
- *⅛ teaspoon pepper*
- *½ teaspoon salt*
- *1 (8-inch) unbaked pie shell*

- Thaw and drain spinach. Combine spinach with next 5 ingredients; mix well. Turn into pie crust and bake 30 minutes at 350°.

*Serve hot or cold. Diced prosciutto or bacon can be added to spinach.*

# *Crustless Crab Quiche*

*The combination of wonderful flavors makes this quiche a hit at any meal.*

- *½ pound fresh mushrooms, sliced*
- *4 scallions, chopped*
- *2 tablespoons butter*
- *4 eggs*
- *1 cup sour cream*
- *1 cup cottage cheese (do not substitute low-fat)*
- *½ cup grated Parmesan cheese*
- *¼ cup flour*
- *¼ teaspoon salt*
- *4 drops bottled hot pepper sauce*
- *½ pound Monterey Jack cheese, grated*
- *6 ounces crabmeat*

- Sauté mushrooms and onions in butter; drain off excess liquid. In a food processor or blender, blend eggs, sour cream, cottage cheese, Parmesan cheese, flour, salt, and hot pepper sauce. Pour into a large bowl. Stir in mushrooms and onions, Monterey Jack cheese, and crabmeat. Pour into a lightly-buttered 10-inch pie plate or shallow casserole.
- Bake at 350° for 45 minutes. Let stand 5 to 10 minutes before serving.

*This is great as an hors d'oeuvre. It can be cut into small squares, frozen, and reheated.*

## *Classic Crêpe Batter*

*So versatile!*

*4 eggs*
*1/4 teaspoon salt*
*2 cups flour*
*2 1/4 cups milk*
*1/4 cup butter, melted*

*Makes 32 to 36 crêpes*

- Combine ingredients in a blender; process about 1 minute. Scrape sides with a rubber spatula; blend another 15 seconds, or until smooth.
- Refrigerate batter at least 1 hour.
- Pour enough batter into an omelette pan so that bottom of heated pan is just covered. Crêpe should be thin. Cook over medium-high heat. Crêpe will be done when batter appears dry and edges begin to curl. Remove crêpe from pan and keep warm. Repeat with remaining batter.

## *Quiche Cups*

*An extra-special presentation of a classic*

*12 cooked crêpes*
*4 slices bacon*
*1 cup grated Swiss cheese*
*2 tablespoons flour*
*1/4 teaspoon salt*
*2 eggs, beaten*
*1 cup milk*

*Makes 12 crêpe cups*

- Line greased muffin pans or custard cups with cooked crêpes.
- Cook bacon until crisp; drain and crumble. Sprinkle into crêpe shells. Top with cheese.
- Mix flour, salt, and eggs with milk; pour over cheese.
- Bake at 350° for 15 to 20 minutes, or until firm. Cool 5 minutes before removing from pan. Serve hot.

# *Old Tavern Crêpes*

*Everyone will want "just one more."*

- *3 tablespoons butter*
- *1 small onion, finely chopped*
- *1 cup sliced fresh mushrooms*
- *¾ cup beer*
- *¼ cup light cream*
- *½ cup julienned cooked ham*
- *1 tablespoon cornstarch*
- *2 tablespoons cold water*
- *salt and pepper to taste*
- *2 cups grated Swiss cheese*
- *10 cooked crêpes*

*Makes 10 crêpes*

- In a skillet, melt butter; add onion and mushrooms. Cook over medium heat for several minutes. Stir in beer, then cream and ham. Simmer 2 to 3 minutes.
- Dissolve cornstarch in 2 tablespoons cold water; add to mushroom mixture. Season with salt and pepper. Cook over low heat until mixture thickens. Stir in 1 cup grated cheese.
- Place several spoonfuls of filling in center of each crêpe. Fold crêpes in half and place in a shallow baking pan. Sprinkle with remaining cup of cheese. Broil until cheese melts.

# *Orange Blush Crêpes*

*Spectacular and scrumptious*

- 3 *ounces cream cheese, softened*
- 1 *tablespoon milk*
- 1/4 *teaspoon vanilla*
- 1/4 *cup finely chopped toasted almonds*
- 6-8 *cooked crêpes*
- 1/4 *cup butter*
- 1/3 *cup sugar*
- 1 *teaspoon lemon juice*
- 2 *teaspoons cornstarch*
- 1/2 *cup freshly squeezed orange juice*
- 1/4 *cup orange liqueur*
- 1 *teaspoon grated orange peel*
- 2 *tablespoons cognac, warmed*
- 2 *tablespoons toasted sliced almonds*
- *orange sections for garnish*

*Makes 6 to 8 crêpes*

- Mix cream cheese with milk and vanilla. Add finely chopped almonds. Spread into center of cooked crêpes. Roll up and set aside.
- Melt butter in a large skillet or chafing dish. Stir in sugar and lemon juice. Dissolve cornstarch in orange juice. Add orange juice, orange liqueur, and grated peel to butter. Cook over low heat, stirring constantly, until thick and translucent. Add filled crêpes to skillet or chafing dish; heat crêpes.
- Pour warm cognac over all. Ignite with a long match. Spoon flaming sauce over crêpes. Garnish with toasted sliced almonds and orange sections. Serve immediately.

# PASTA & SAUCES

*Pasta and Sauces*

## *Spaghetti with Mushroom Champagne Sauce*

*Consider candlelight when serving this elegant pasta meal.*

- ½ *pound fresh mushrooms, sliced*
- 1 *clove garlic, minced*
- 1 *teaspoon tomato paste*
- ¼ *cup heavy cream*
- 8 *ounces spaghetti or fettucine, cooked and drained*
- 1 *cup champagne*
- 2 *tablespoons olive oil*
- *chopped fresh parsley for garnish*

- Sauté garlic in olive oil. Add mushrooms and cook until soft. Add champagne and reduce by half. Add tomato paste, then cream. Pour over spaghetti and garnish with fresh parsley.

## *Linguine with Pesto Sauce*

*Snip some basil from your garden to make this popular pasta.*

- 1 *cup loosely packed fresh basil leaves*
- 2 *cloves garlic*
- ¼ *cup pine nuts*
- ¾ *cup grated Parmesan cheese*
- ½ *cup olive oil*
- 8 *ounces linguine, cooked and drained*

- Blend basil leaves, garlic, and pine nuts in a food processor or blender. Add grated Parmesan cheese; blend. With blender on, add olive oil in a slow, steady stream.
- Toss cooked pasta with pesto sauce. Serve immediately.

*Olive oil can be warmed prior to adding to herb/cheese mixture.*

*Do not reheat on stove as sauce will separate. If reheating is desired, microwave until warm.*

# *Goat Cheese Ravioli with Garlic Tomato Sauce*

*When you taste this, you'll know that it is well worth the effort.*

- *3/4 pound mild goat cheese*
- *3 tablespoons cottage cheese*
- *1/3 cup finely chopped prosciutto*
- *1/4 cup finely chopped fresh basil*
- *1/2 teaspoon finely grated lemon zest*
- *1 egg, beaten*
- *1 egg mixed with 1 tablespoon water (egg wash)*
- *salt and pepper to taste*
- *60 won ton wrappers*

## *Sauce*

- *1/4 cup olive oil*
- *1 (28 ounce) can plum tomatoes, drained and finely chopped*
- *1 1/2 teaspoons fresh thyme*
- *3 large cloves garlic, finely chopped*

- Combine goat cheese, cottage cheese, prosciutto, basil, lemon zest, and egg. Mix well; add salt and pepper to taste. Chill at least 1 hour.
- Prepare sauce by heating oil in a heavy skillet. Add tomatoes and thyme. Bring to a boil. Add garlic. Simmer uncovered until sauce has thickened. Keep warm.
- Place a single won ton wrapper on work surface. Brush lightly with egg wash. Place 1 tablespoon of filling in center. Place second won ton on top. Press down to eliminate air. If desired, crimp or cut edges using a fancy cookie cutter. As ravioli are formed, place on a kitchen towel to dry, turning occasionally.
- Cook ravioli in boiling, salted water for 2 minutes, or until they rise to the surface.
- Drain water from cooked ravioli. Serve with prepared sauce.

*Quantity of cottage cheese can be increased. Ricotta cheese is a tasty alternative.*

# *Pasta Alfredo Di Contessa*

*Fit for the royalty at your family's table*

- *8 ounces each linguine and capellini (called Hay and Straw when combined)*
- *1/4 cup butter*
- *1/4 teaspoon garlic powder*
- *1 pint heavy cream*
- *1 tablespoon cornstarch*
- *8 tablespoons grated Locatelli, Romano, or Parmesan cheese*
- *freshly ground pepper*

• Cook pasta in boiling water until "al dente." Drain.

• While pasta is cooking, sauté garlic in butter in a small saucepan. Do not allow garlic to brown; cook only until translucent. Reduce heat.

• In a separate bowl, mix cornstarch and cream. Add mixture, slowly, to saucepan and heat until thickened, stirring constantly. Do not allow to boil. Add cheese and cook until well blended.

• Toss pasta with sauce. Serve with more grated cheese and freshly ground pepper, to taste.

# *Pasta Primavera*

*A perfect mix of all that is delicious in spring*

- 2 *tablespoons olive oil*
- ½ *red pepper, julienned*
- 1 *cup broccoli flowerets*
- 1 *carrot, julienned*
- ½ *pound fresh mushrooms, sliced*
- 1 *teaspoon basil*
- 1 *teaspoon minced fresh parsley*
- *pasta (spaghetti, linguine, or fettucine)*

## *Sauce*

- 6 *tablespoons butter*
- 1 *cup heavy cream*
- ½ *cup grated Parmesan cheese*
- 1 *clove garlic, minced*

- Stir-fry vegetables in olive oil. Season with basil and parsley. Turn off heat. Cover to keep warm.
- While pasta is cooking, prepare sauce. Melt butter; add cream, cheese, and garlic. Cook until cheese is melted. Toss vegetables, pasta, and sauce together.

## *Lemon Fettucine*

*Tangy!*

- *3/4 pound fettucine (half egg, half spinach)*
- *2 lemons*
- *1 cup heavy cream*
- *salt and freshly ground pepper to taste*

- With a vegetable peeler, carefully remove outermost layer of yellow rind from lemons in long strips. Cut into thin strips and set aside.
- Squeeze juice from lemons into a saucepan with cream, salt, and pepper. Allow cream sauce to boil for 1 minute. Reduce heat; simmer.
- Boil fettucine in salted water until pasta is "al dente." Toss with hot cream sauce.
- Top each portion with julienned lemon rind and freshly ground pepper.

## *Parmesan Cheese Sauce*

*Over the centuries, hundreds of pasta shapes have evolved. This sauce will complement any of them.*

- *8 ounces cream cheese, cubed*
- *3/4 cup milk*
- *1/2 cup grated Parmesan cheese*
- *dash of nutmeg*
- *dash of freshly ground pepper*

- Microwave cream cheese, milk, and Parmesan cheese in a bowl on medium for 6 to 8 minutes, or until sauce is smooth, stirring every 2 minutes. Stir in seasonings. Toss with hot, cooked pasta.

## *Spaghetti Putanesca*

*An Italian masterpiece*

- 4 *tablespoons olive oil*
- 1 *cup diced ripe tomatoes*
- ¼ *cup Sicilian olives, pitted*
- 1 *can anchovies*
- ¼ *cup capers*
- 2-3 *cloves garlic, minced*
- *freshly ground pepper to taste*
- *pasta (spaghetti, linguine, or fettucine)*
- *Romano cheese to taste*

- Heat oil. Add all ingredients and simmer.
- Boil pasta in salted water until "al dente." Drain. Serve with sauce. Sprinkle with grated cheese.

## *Sunday Spaghetti Sauce*

*The aroma will entice you to sample this sauce again and again and again...*

- 1 *pound ground round*
- 1 *(29 ounce) can tomato purée*
- 1 *(29 ounce) can whole tomatoes*
- 1 *(6 ounce) can tomato paste*
- 2 *tablespoons parsley*
- 2 *tablespoons oregano*
- 2-3 *cloves garlic, chopped*
- ¼ *cup sugar*
- 1-2 *onions, chopped*
- 1 *tablespoon celery salt*
- 3 *tablespoons basil*
- 4 *tablespoons red wine*
- *salt and pepper to taste*

- Brown ground round with garlic. Drain off fat.
- Add tomato paste and continue browning. Add sugar to browning paste.
- Add all remaining ingredients. After mixture has come to a boil, lower heat so that sauce can simmer 2 to 2½ hours. Stir occasionally.

## *20-Minute Homemade Spaghetti Sauce*

*All of the flavor, half of the time*

- *½ cup chopped onion*
- *1 clove garlic, crushed*
- *1 tablespoon vegetable oil*
- *1 (14½ ounce) can whole tomatoes*
- *2 (6 ounce) cans tomato paste*
- *1 cup water*
- *1 beef bouillon cube*
- *1 tablespoon grated Parmesan cheese*
- *1 tablespoon sugar*
- *½ teaspoon each basil, oregano, and salt*
- *⅛ teaspoon pepper*

- In a heavy saucepan, sauté onion and garlic in oil until tender.
- Add remaining ingredients; mix thoroughly.
- Simmer covered, 15 minutes, stirring occasionally.

*For a sure-to-be-popular variation, sauté 1 cup sliced fresh mushrooms in oil with onion and garlic. Or, sauté onion and garlic with ½ pound Italian sausage or ground beef instead of oil.*

## *Local Favorite Pasta Sauce*

*You couldn't legislate a quicker, tastier recipe than this one from New York State Senator Tom Libous.*

- *olive oil*
- *8 ounces prosciutto, chopped*
- *1 cup chopped scallions*
- *1 clove garlic, minced*
- *3 (14½ ounce) cans whole tomatoes*
- *salt and pepper*
- *½ cup dried parsley*
- *cooked pasta*

- Cover bottom of a saucepan with olive oil. Heat gently. Add prosciutto, scallions, and garlic. Simmer for 10 minutes. Crush tomatoes and add to pan. Season with salt, pepper, and parsley. Simmer for 20 minutes. (Sauce should remain thin.) Serve over cooked pasta.

## *Pasta with Chicken and Peppers*

*Family and friends alike will rave about this special dish.*

- 2 *tablespoons olive oil*
- 6 *cloves garlic*
- 1 *small red onion, sliced*
- 1 *yellow bell pepper, sliced*
- 2 *scallions, sliced*
- ¼ *teaspoon cayenne pepper*
- 1½ *cups sliced chicken breast*
- 12 *ounces ziti*
- 2 *bunches escarole, cut lengthwise*
- ¼ *teaspoon nutmeg*
- ¼ *teaspoon pepper*
- ½ *cup grated Parmesan cheese*

- Sauté garlic, onion, pepper, and scallions in olive oil. Add chicken and cook until brown (5 to 10 minutes); set aside.
- Boil pasta 6 to 8 minutes in salted water. Add escarole and cook an additional 4 to 5 minutes. Drain, reserving 1 cup liquid.
- Combine chicken and vegetables with cooked pasta. Add reserved liquid and season with nutmeg and pepper. Sprinkle with grated Parmesan cheese.

## *Penne Rigate with Chicken*

*That's Italian!*

- ⅓ *cup olive oil*
- 3 *cloves garlic, minced*
- 2 *whole boneless chicken breasts*
- 1 *green bell pepper, julienned*
- 1 *red bell pepper, julienned*
- 2 *carrots, julienned*
- 10 *fresh mushrooms, thickly sliced*
- *salt and pepper to taste*
- 1 *pound Penne Rigate or any tubular pasta, cooked and drained*
- *grated Parmesan cheese*

- Heat oil and garlic in a large frying pan. Cook chicken until lightly browned. Remove from pan and set aside.
- Quickly stir-fry green and red peppers, carrots, and mushrooms in hot oil so that they retain their crunch. Salt and pepper to taste. Return chicken to pan, briefly, to warm.
- Pour sauce over cooked pasta. Serve with grated cheese.

# *Spaghetti with Smoked Salmon and Watercress*

*A unique combination for the sophisticated palate*

- 8 *ounces spaghetti*
- $1\frac{1}{2}$ *teaspoons olive oil*
- 1 *clove garlic, minced*
- 2 *ounces smoked salmon, julienned*
- 1 *bunch watercress, washed and stemmed*
- *freshly ground pepper*

- Boil spaghetti in 3 quarts salted water until "al dente."
- Just before spaghetti finishes cooking, heat oil in a large skillet over medium heat. Add garlic and cook 30 seconds, stirring constantly.
- Add salmon, watercress, and pepper; cook 30 seconds. Remove skillet from heat.
- Drain spaghetti and add to skillet. Toss with sauce and serve immediately.

## *Linguine with Clam Sauce*

*An exceptional rendition of a traditional favorite*

- 1/2 *cup butter*
- 1/2 *cup olive oil*
- 1 *teaspoon Dijon mustard*
- 2 *large cloves garlic, minced*
- 3-5 *scallions, chopped*
- 1/4 *cup chopped fresh parsley*
- 1/4 *teaspoon oregano*
- 1 *tablespoon lemon juice*
- 1 *pound frozen clams, thawed and chopped*
- *freshly ground pepper to taste*
- *fettucine or linguine*
- 6-8 *ounces broccoli, steamed*
- *grated Parmesan cheese*

- In a saucepan, melt butter; add oil and mustard. Sauté garlic and scallions, but do not brown.
- Add oregano, parsley, and lemon juice. Lower heat and add clams. Cook clams over low heat until done, but not rubbery. Season with pepper to taste.
- Place cooked pasta in a serving bowl. Add warm broccoli. Cover with clam sauce. Toss lightly and serve at once. Sprinkle with grated Parmesan cheese.

## *Make Ahead Macaroni*

*Even the children will come back for more.*

- 1 *pound cut ziti, cooked and drained*
- 1 *pound ricotta cheese*
- 1 *egg*
- 2 1/2 *cups spaghetti sauce*
- 1/2 *cup grated Romano cheese*
- 4 *ounces mozzarella cheese, grated*

- Combine cooked ziti, ricotta cheese, egg, spaghetti sauce, and Romano cheese in a casserole. Top with mozzarella cheese.
- Cover with foil, punching 3 or 4 holes in top for escaping steam. Bake in a 350° oven for 45 minutes.

*Macaroni can be prepared in advance. Complement with salad and crusty Italian bread.*

# FOWL & FARE

# FOWL & FARE



## *Chicken*



## *Ducks, Hens, and Turkey*

## *Lemon Garlic Chicken*

*The choice of the Junior League of Binghamton at its own special affairs...*

- *4-5 cloves garlic, minced*
- *olive oil for browning*
- *3-4 pounds boneless chicken breast*
- *3-4 eggs*
- *bread crumbs (1/4-1/2 cup per pound chicken)*
- *1 cup chicken broth*
- *1/2 cup white wine*
- *juice from one lemon*
- *sliced lemon for garnish*
- *1/4 cup grated Parmesan cheese*
- *salt and pepper to taste*

*Serves 10 to 12*

- Sauté minced garlic in olive oil. Bread chicken with egg and crumbs. Brown, and drain on paper towels.
- Place chicken in a casserole dish and sprinkle with lemon juice. Add chicken broth and white wine and top with lemon slices and Parmesan cheese. Bake at 350° for 1 hour.

## *Champagne Chicken*

*Simply sublime*

- *4 shallots, chopped*
- *4 boneless chicken breasts*
- *3 tablespoons butter*
- *2 cups champagne*
- *12 ounces fresh mushrooms, sliced*
- *1/2 teaspoon tarragon*
- *1 cup heavy cream*
- *2 tablespoons flour*
- *salt and pepper to taste*

*Serves 4*

- Sauté chicken and shallots in butter until chicken is no longer pink inside. Add tarragon, champagne, and mushrooms. Simmer until liquid has been reduced by half.
- Add heavy cream and flour. Simmer, stirring constantly, until thickened.

## *"Rush-in" Chicken*

*"What's for dinner, Mom?"*

*1 small jar apricot preserves*
*1 bottle red Russian salad dressing*
*1 envelope dried onion soup mix*
*1½-2½ pounds boneless chicken breasts*

*Serves 6 to 8*

- Combine preserves, dressing, and soup mix.
- Coat chicken with sauce and place in a baking dish in a single layer. Cover chicken with remaining sauce. Cover and bake at 350° for 25 to 35 minutes.

## *No Work Chicken*

*Great to have ready when you come home from work*

*4 boneless chicken breasts*
*½ cup honey*
*½ cup Dijon mustard*
*1 tablespoon curry powder*
*2 tablespoons soy sauce*

*Serves 4*

- Place chicken in a flat baking dish in a single layer.
- Prepare marinade by mixing together honey, mustard, curry powder, and soy sauce. Pour over chicken and refrigerate for 6 hours, or overnight.
- Turn chicken, cover dish with foil, and bake at 350° for 1 hour.
- Remove foil, baste well, and continue baking, uncovered, for 15 more minutes. When serving, spoon sauce over chicken.

## *Swiss Bliss*

*Deliver this dish as a warm welcome to a new neighbor.*

- *8 boneless chicken breasts*
- *3/4 pound Swiss cheese, sliced*
- *1 can condensed cream of celery soup*
- *1/4 cup sherry*
- *1 1/2 cups crushed seasoned stuffing mix*
- *3 tablespoons butter*

• Arrange chicken in a greased shallow baking dish. Place cheese slices over chicken. Mix condensed soup with sherry. Pour over chicken and cheese. Sprinkle with stuffing mix and dot with butter. Bake at 350° for 1 hour.

*Serves 6 to 8*

## *Chicken Dijon*

*The mustard gives this quick recipe a "company flair."*

- *8 boneless chicken breasts*
- *3 tablespoons butter*
- *2 tablespoons flour*
- *1 cup chicken broth*
- *1/2 cup light cream*
- *2 tablespoons Dijon mustard*
- *tomato wedges for garnish*
- *parsley for garnish*

• In a large skillet, cook breasts in butter approximately 20 minutes. Remove chicken to a warm platter. Stir flour into drippings. Add broth and cream. Cook and stir until mixture thickens and bubbles. Stir in mustard. Add chicken, cover, and heat 10 minutes. Garnish with tomato and parsley.

*Serves 8*

## *Pecan Fried Chicken*

*Raise fried chicken to company standards.*

- 8 *boneless chicken breasts*
- 1½ *teaspoons salt*
- 1 *teaspoon pepper*
- 1 *teaspoon paprika*
- ¾ *cup butter*
- 12 *ounces pecans, ground*
- 6 *tablespoons Dijon mustard*
- ¼ *cup vegetable oil*
- 1 *cup sour cream*

*Serves 8*

- Flatten chicken breasts. Mix salt, pepper, paprika, and pecans in a bowl. In a saucepan, melt ½ cup butter; whisk in 3 tablespoons mustard. Dip chicken in mustard, then pecan mixture; let set for 10 to 15 minutes.
- Melt ¼ cup butter in a large electric skillet. Add oil and heat to 350°. Sauté breasts until done; keep warm on a platter in a 200° oven.
- Deglaze skillet with sour cream and remaining mustard. Serve sauce over breasts.

## *Crunchy Wheat Drumsticks*

*For the health conscious*

- 8 *chicken drumsticks*
- ⅓ *cup Dijon mustard*
- 1 *egg white*
- 1 *teaspoon lemon juice*
- 1 *cup whole-wheat bread crumbs (4 slices stale, whole-wheat bread)*
- ½ *teaspoon basil*
- 1 *tablespoon olive oil*

*Serves 4*

- Lightly grease a 15x10x1½-inch jelly roll pan or spray with non-stick vegetable oil.
- Remove skin from chicken; pat chicken dry.
- Combine mustard, egg white, and lemon juice in a shallow dish. Combine bread crumbs and basil on a piece of waxed paper. Dip chicken pieces in mustard mixture, turning to coat. Then, dip in bread crumbs. Place on prepared pan. Drizzle with oil.
- Bake at 375° for 35 minutes, or until golden brown and cooked through.

## *Tempting Chicken Tenders*

*Kids love these.*

- 1½ *pounds chicken tenders*
- ¾ *cup butter, melted*
- 2 *cloves garlic, minced*
- 1 *cup fine dry bread crumbs*
- ⅔ *cup grated Parmesan cheese*
- ¼ *cup minced fresh parsley*
- ½ *teaspoon salt*
- ¼ *teaspoon pepper*
- 2 *tablespoons lemon juice*

• Combine butter and garlic; set aside. Combine bread crumbs, cheese, parsley, salt, and pepper. Dip chicken pieces in butter and coat with crumb mixture. Place chicken pieces in a large, greased baking dish in a single layer. Sprinkle remaining crumbs on top. Sprinkle with lemon juice. Bake at 350° for 35 to 40 minutes.

*Serves 4 to 6*

## *Honey Chicken*

*When you need a change — this is simple and tasty.*

- 4 *boneless chicken breasts, cut in strips*
- 4 *tablespoons butter, melted*
- ½ *cup honey*
- 1 *teaspoon curry*
- ¼ *cup Dijon mustard*
- ¼ *teaspoon salt*

• Arrange chicken strips in the bottom of a baking dish.

• Combine remaining ingredients and pour over chicken. Bake at 350° for 45 minutes.

*Serves 4*

## *Grilled Chicken Marinade*

*A welcome change from barbecue sauce*

- *2 eggs*
- *1 cup vegetable oil*
- *2 cups cider vinegar*
- *1 tablespoon salt*
- *1 teaspoon pepper*
- *3 teaspoons poultry seasoning*
- *6-8 pounds chicken pieces*

*Serves 10 to 12*

- Beat eggs until light; add remaining ingredients (except chicken). Beat until well blended.
- Marinate chicken in sauce, refrigerated, for 2 to 24 hours. Grill chicken, basting with marinade each time chicken is turned.

## *Chicken Teriyaki*

*An easy favorite!*

- *1 cup soy sauce*
- *1/4 cup vegetable oil*
- *3 tablespoons garlic powder*
- *2 tablespoons ginger*
- *1/4 cup rice wine*
- *8 boneless chicken breasts*

*Serves 8*

- Combine all ingredients (except chicken). Mix well.
- Marinate chicken in sauce, refrigerated, for 2 to 24 hours. Grill or broil chicken for 3 to 4 minutes on each side. Do not overcook.

# *Calypso Chicken Barbecue*

*Sure to have your guests dancing around the grill*

- 2 *chicken broilers, cut into serving pieces*
- 1/2 *cup butter*
- *salt and pepper to taste*

## *Barbecue Sauce*

- 1/2 *cup olive oil*
- 1 *onion, finely chopped*
- 1 *clove garlic, crushed*
- 2 *cups chili sauce*
- 1 *cup ketchup*
- 1/2 *teaspoon oregano*
- 1/2 *teaspoon celery seed*
- 1 *tablespoon Dijon mustard*
- 1 *tablespoon wine vinegar*
- 1/2 *teaspoon pepper*
- *salt to taste*
- *a few drops bottled hot pepper sauce*
- 1/4 *teaspoon cumin*
- 1/3 *cup dark rum*

*Serves 6 to 8*

- Place chicken in a shallow pan and dot with butter. Sprinkle with salt and paprika. Bake at 350° for 1 hour.
- To prepare barbecue sauce, heat olive oil. In oil, sauté onion and garlic until wilted. Add chili sauce, ketchup, oregano, celery seed, mustard, wine vinegar, pepper, hot pepper sauce (if desired), and cumin. Bring to a boil; reduce heat, simmer 10 minutes. Stir in dark rum.
- When ready to serve, cover chicken with barbecue sauce and broil or grill until crusty and brown.

# *Tarragon Poulet*

*Piquant herbs and seasonings make this distinctive.*

- *8 boneless chicken breasts*
- *2 tablespoons olive oil*
- *4 tablespoons butter*
- *6 shallots, chopped*
- *2 carrots, sliced into 1/4-inch rounds*
- *1/4 cup cognac or brandy*
- *1 cup dry white wine*
- *1/4 cup chopped fresh tarragon (or 2 teaspoons dried)*
- *1 1/2 tablespoons fresh chopped chervil (or 1/2 teaspoon dried)*
- *1/2 teaspoon salt*
- *1/8 teaspoon pepper*
- *1 cup light cream*
- *1 egg yolk*
- *1 tablespoon flour*
- *1/4 pound fresh mushrooms, thinly sliced*
- *sprigs of fresh tarragon for garnish*

*Serves 8*

- In a 6-quart Dutch oven, heat oil and 2 tablespoons butter. Add chicken breasts (half at a time, enough to cover bottom of pan); sauté, turning on all sides, until brown. Remove chicken as it browns.

- To drippings in Dutch oven, add shallots and carrots; sauté, stirring 5 minutes, or until golden. Return chicken to Dutch oven; heat. When chicken is hot, heat cognac in ladle over gas flame or electric burner; ignite. Pour, flaming, over chicken. Add wine, chopped tarragon, chervil, salt, and pepper.

- Bring to boiling; reduce heat and simmer gently, covered, 30 minutes. Remove chicken to a heated serving platter; keep warm. Strain drippings, discarding vegetables; return drippings to Dutch oven.

- In a small bowl, combine cream, egg yolk and flour; mix well with a wire whisk. Stir into drippings in Dutch oven. Bring just to boiling, stirring constantly. Add more wine if sauce seems too thick. Meanwhile, sauté mushrooms in hot butter until tender. Spoon sauce over chicken. Garnish with tarragon and mushrooms.

## *Chicken with Wine and Vegetables*

*Tom Selleck's favorite chicken has become one of our favorites too!*

- *8 boneless chicken breasts*
- *1 onion, sliced*
- *3 tablespoons butter*
- *salt and pepper*
- *½ cup flour*
- *8 whole fresh mushrooms*
- *1 cup orange juice*
- *1 cup Marsala wine*
- *¼ cup ginger ale*
- *2 tablespoons lemon juice*
- *1 can artichoke hearts*
- *hot cooked brown rice*

*Serves 6 to 8*

- Brown onions in 1 tablespoon butter; set aside.
- Salt and pepper chicken after washing. Dredge in flour. Brown quickly in remaining butter.
- Place onions in bottom of a Dutch oven. Cover onions with a layer of chicken and mushrooms. Combine liquid ingredients; pour over chicken. Cook, covered, at 325° for 1 hour. Add artichoke hearts; cook for an additional 30 minutes. Serve with brown rice.

## *Chicken Breasts Chablis*

*Special but easy to prepare after a busy day.*

- *8 boneless chicken breasts*
- *flour*
- *2 eggs, beaten*
- *seasoned bread crumbs*
- *vegetable oil for frying*
- *½ cup butter*
- *1 (4 ounce) can mushrooms*
- *1 cup Chablis wine*

*Serves 6*

- Flour each chicken breast, dip in egg, then in seasoned bread crumbs. Fry chicken in oil until golden brown; drain on paper towels then place in baking dish.
- In a saucepan, melt butter. Add mushrooms and wine; bring to a boil for 2 minutes. Pour mixture over chicken, cover and bake at 350° for 45 to 60 minutes.

# *Algerian Chicken*

*When you are feeling adventurous...*

- *2 medium onions, thinly sliced and separated into rings*
- *1 medium green pepper, cut into thin strips*
- *3/4 cup sliced fresh mushrooms*
- *1 tablespoon water*
- *2 teaspoons oregano*
- *2 teaspoons crushed red pepper*
- *1 teaspoon garlic salt*
- *1/2 teaspoon bottled hot pepper sauce*
- *1 (14 1/2 ounce) can tomatoes*
- *2/3 cup peanut butter*
- *2 teaspoons instant chicken bouillon granules*
- *8 boneless, skinless chicken breasts*
- *hot cooked rice*

*Serves 8*

- In a medium saucepan, combine onions, green pepper, mushrooms, water, oregano, red pepper, garlic salt, and hot pepper sauce. Cook over medium heat, stirring frequently, until vegetables are crisp-tender.
- In a blender or food processor, combine undrained tomatoes, peanut butter, and bouillon granules. Blend or process until smooth.
- Rinse chicken; pat dry. Place in a 13x9x2-inch baking dish. Top with vegetable mixture. Pour tomato mixture over all. Cover and bake in a 350° oven for 45 to 55 minutes, or until chicken is tender. Transfer chicken to a serving platter or individual plates; stir sauce and spoon on top. Serve with rice.

# *Chicken with Peanuts, Cabbage, and Red Peppers (Sui-mi Ji)*

*An authentic stir-fry, sure to spice up your life*

- *1 pound boneless chicken breast, cut into small pieces*
- *½ head cabbage, coarsely chopped*
- *3 tablespoons cornstarch*
- *3 tablespoons rice wine*
- *2 tablespoons vinegar*
- *2 tablespoons soy sauce*
- *½ cup crushed peanuts*
- *3-4 dried hot red peppers, slivered and seeds removed*
- *3 cloves garlic, minced*
- *1 tablespoon chopped fresh ginger root*
- *3 scallions, coarsely chopped*
- *¼ teaspoon salt*
- *¼ teaspoon sugar*
- *2 teaspoons sesame oil*
- *¾ cup vegetable oil*
- *1 tablespoon hot bean sauce*

*Serves 6*

- Prepare marinade by mixing 2 tablespoons each of cornstarch, rice wine, vinegar, and soy sauce. Mix with chicken and marinate at least 15 minutes.

- Combine remaining cornstarch and rice wine, salt, sugar, and sesame oil to make a seasoning mix. Set aside.

- Heat 6 tablespoons vegetable oil in a wok until hot. Add cabbage; stir-fry quickly. When cabbage softens and appears slightly cooked, remove from heat and drain. Arrange on a serving platter, leaving space in center.

- Heat additional oil in wok until very hot. Add chicken pieces; cook quickly. When chicken is white, add ginger, garlic, scallions, peanuts, and peppers. Stir briefly; add hot bean sauce. Cook, stirring, another 10 to 15 seconds. Stir seasonings and add to wok. Serve over bed of cabbage.

*Dish reheats well and leftovers make a good base for fried rice.*

## *Spicy Chicken*

*Elizabeth Taylor is "passion"-ate about this dish; you will be too.*

- *2 teaspoons curry powder*
- *1 teaspoon cumin*
- *½ teaspoon ginger*
- *½ teaspoon turmeric*
- *½ clove garlic, crushed*
- *1 onion, chopped*
- *1 teaspoon grated fresh ginger root*
- *1 medium chicken, cut into serving pieces and skinned*

- Combine dry ingredients with garlic, onion, and fresh ginger. Coat chicken with mixture and refrigerate for at least 2 hours, preferably longer.
- Place on a moderately hot barbecue grill or broil in oven 30 minutes, turning once.

*Serves 4*

## *Broiled Chicken with Cucumber Sauce*

*Light, yet truly satisfying*

- *½ cup olive oil*
- *¼ cup lemon juice*
- *1 cup dry white wine*
- *1 teaspoon oregano*
- *1 broiler-fryer (approximately 2½ pounds), split and quartered*
- *1 cup plain yogurt*
- *1 clove garlic, crushed*
- *1 teaspoon salt*
- *1 cucumber, peeled, seeded, and finely chopped*

- Combine ¼ cup olive oil, lemon juice, wine and oregano. Pour over chicken in a baking dish. Marinate at room temperature for 3 hours.
- Prepare cucumber sauce by combining yogurt, remaining olive oil, garlic, salt, and cucumber.
- Broil or grill chicken, turning once and basting with marinade, until done. Serve with cucumber sauce.

*Serves 4*

# *Feta Stuffed Chicken Breast with Greek Salsa*

*Out of this world!*

- *4 boneless chicken breasts*
- *2 tablespoons crumbled feta cheese*
- *1 tablespoon chopped walnuts*
- *1 tablespoon chopped fresh parsley*
- *3/4 cup flour*
- *salt and pepper to taste*
- *1 egg*
- *2 tablespoons milk*
- *2 tablespoons olive oil*
- *2 tablespoons butter*

## *Greek Salsa*

- *3 tablespoons olive oil*
- *1/2 cup each chopped onion, carrots, and celery*
- *2 cloves garlic, chopped*
- *2 (8 ounce) cans tomatoes, drained and chopped*
- *4 tablespoons chopped fresh parsley*
- *1/2 cup white wine*
- *1/2 teaspoon sugar*
- *1/2 teaspoon oregano*

*Serves 4*

- Cut a slit in each chicken cutlet (taking care not to cut all the way through) to create a small pocket.
- Mix feta cheese, walnuts, and parsley. Put 1 tablespoon of stuffing in each cutlet and seal edges by pressing together. Mix flour, salt, and pepper. Dredge cutlets in flour mixture. Mix egg and milk. Dip cutlets in egg mixture and then again in flour mixture. Refrigerate until ready to cook.
- Heat olive oil and butter in a large, heavy skillet, over medium heat, until foam subsides. Cook cutlets over medium-high heat until brown. Turn cutlets over and reduce heat. Cook until brown and cooked through. Do not cover, as the chicken will lose its crispness and the cheese will begin to ooze out of the cutlet.
- To prepare salsa, heat olive oil in a small, heavy skillet. Cook onion, carrots, celery, and garlic until limp. Add drained tomatoes, parsley, wine, sugar, and oregano. Simmer for 20 minutes, or until thick. Serve over chicken.

*The vegetable-laden salsa makes a memorable meal of a broiled chicken breast. You can also please your family with simply the feta-stuffed chicken.*

## *Rosemary Chicken with Orange Sauce*

*This saucy dish is always a hit with last-minute guests.*

- *6 chicken breasts (with bone or boneless)*
- *salt and pepper*
- *2 teaspoons rosemary*
- *1/4 cup butter*
- *2 tablespoons flour*
- *1 (6 ounce) can frozen orange juice concentrate*
- *1 (10 1/2 ounce) can condensed chicken broth*
- *1 (11 ounce) can Mandarin orange sections, drained*
- *orange slices for garnish*

- Sprinkle chicken with salt, pepper, and rosemary. Heat butter in a skillet and brown chicken slowly on all sides. Cook about 20 minutes, or until done. Remove from pan and keep warm.
- Stir flour into drippings. Add juice concentrate and broth. Cook, stirring occasionally, until mixture is thickened. Season to taste with salt. Gently blend in orange sections and pour over chicken. Serve with a fresh orange slice twist for garnish.

*Serves 6*

## *Chicken Florentine*

*An excellent rendition of a traditional favorite*

- *5 (10 ounce) packages frozen spinach*
- *1/2 teaspoon lemon juice*
- *1/2 pound fresh mushrooms*
- *6 tablespoons butter*
- *4 whole chicken breasts*
- *1/4 cup flour*
- *1 teaspoon salt*
- *1/4 teaspoon pepper*
- *1 cup chicken broth*
- *1 cup heavy cream*
- *1/2 cup grated Parmesan cheese*

- Cook spinach according to directions on package; cool. Squeeze spinach very dry and arrange in bottom of a buttered 9x13-inch baking dish. Sprinkle with lemon juice.
- Chop mushrooms and sauté in 2 tablespoons butter until limp.
- Melt remaining butter. Dip chicken in butter; dredge in flour. Arrange chicken over spinach, cover with mushrooms, and sprinkle with salt and pepper. Pour chicken broth and cream over all and top with cheese. Bake at 400° for 20 minutes.

*Serves 6 to 8*

# *Pollo Alla Cacciatore*

*An easy way to impress your family*

- *1 (4 pound) roasting chicken*
- *1/4 cup olive oil*
- *1/2 cup sliced onion*
- *3/4 cup chopped green peppers*
- *2 cloves garlic, minced*
- *2 pounds Italian plum tomatoes, peeled and mashed (juice reserved)*
- *2 tablespoons minced fresh parsley*
- *3/4 teaspoon oregano*
- *1/2 teaspoon thyme*
- *1 teaspoon salt*
- *1/2 teaspoon pepper*
- *1/2 pound fresh mushrooms, sliced*
- *1/4 cup Marsala wine*

*Serves 4*

- Cut chicken into serving pieces. Heat oil in a large fryer. Brown chicken pieces well; remove from pan.
- Add onion, green pepper, and garlic and sauté over medium heat until onion is tender. Add tomatoes and their juice, parsley, oregano, thyme, salt, and pepper. Cook over very low heat for 15 minutes.
- Return browned chicken to pan and cook slowly, covered, over low heat for about 45 minutes. Stir occasionally. Add mushrooms and wine. Cook, uncovered, to reduce sauce to desired consistency (about 15 minutes). Remove chicken pieces to a deep platter. Serve with tomato sauce.

# *Cider Baked Chicken with Apples*

*A trip to the cider mill is an autumn tradition.*

- *2 (3 pound) chickens, skinned and quartered*
- *2 cups apple cider*
- *1 cup flour*
- *1 tablespoon ginger*
- *2 teaspoons cinnamon*
- *salt and pepper to taste*
- *1 large onion, chopped*
- *3 tablespoons brown sugar*
- *1/3 cup applejack or brandy*
- *2 apples, cored and cut into thin wedges*
- *1 tablespoon butter*

*Serves 6*

- Place chicken pieces in a shallow dish. Pour cider over chicken and marinate overnight, covered and refrigerated, turning pieces occasionally.
- Remove chicken from dish, reserving cider. Melt butter in a small frying pan; sauté onion. Remove from heat. Combine onion with cider, brown sugar, applejack, and apple slices. Set aside.
- Combine flour, ginger, cinnamon, salt, and pepper. Dredge chicken in flour mixture. Place chicken in a shallow baking pan and bake at 350° for 40 minutes.
- Pour marinade mixture over chicken and bake 25 minutes more, basting chicken occasionally with pan juices. Serve at once.

# *Roast Chicken in Fragrant Spices*

*A hint of mint does great things for chicken.*

- *1 (3 pound) roasting chicken*
- *2 cloves garlic, pressed*
- *2 teaspoons grated fresh ginger root*
- *2 teaspoons curry powder*
- *1 teaspoon paprika*
- *1 teaspoon salt*
- *½ teaspoon pepper*
- *1 teaspoon lemon juice*
- *2 teaspoons light soy sauce*
- *2 tablespoons vegetable oil*
- *2 tablespoons ground rice*
- *warm water*
- *2 tablespoons finely chopped scallion*
- *1 tablespoon chopped fresh parsley*
- *1 tablespoon chopped fresh mint*

*Serves 4*

- Wash and dry chicken. Combine all other ingredients with sufficient warm water to make a paste of spreading consistency. Rub paste inside and outside chicken. Let stand for 1 hour.
- Roast in a 350° oven for 1¼ hours, or until chicken is done and juices run clear. If bird browns too much during roasting, cover with foil.

*This can be served warm or cold.*

# *Duck à l'Orange*

*The definitive holiday meal*

*1 (3-4 pound) duckling, quartered*
*¼ cup freshly squeezed orange juice*
*salt and pepper*
*1 tablespoon butter*
*¼ cup finely chopped onion*
*1½ tablespoons flour*
*⅔ cup dry red wine*
*⅔ cup chicken broth*
*3 tablespoons orange marmalade*
*1 teaspoon cider vinegar*
*1 teaspoon lemon zest*
*thinly slivered orange peel, optional*
*fresh mint sprigs, optional*

*Serves 4*

- Trim duck quarters of excess skin, bone, and fat. Using a small sharp knife, prick skin well all over duck. Rub orange juice into duck; sprinkle with salt and pepper. Place duck quarters, skin-side down, on rack in a roasting pan. Roast at 450° for 30 minutes, turning duck and pricking skin again after 20 minutes.

- While duck roasts, in an 8-inch skillet over medium heat, melt butter. Add onion; cook about 5 minutes, stirring occasionally, until softened. Add flour; cook 3 minutes, stirring constantly. Stir in wine and chicken broth; increase heat to medium-high and bring to a boil, stirring. Reduce heat to medium and simmer 5 to 7 minutes, stirring occasionally until mixture is slightly thickened. Remove from heat and stir in marmalade, vinegar, lemon zest, ½ teaspoon salt and ¼ teaspoon pepper. Baste duck generously with sauce and roast 5 minutes longer.

- Adjust oven setting to broil; move oven rack to 6 inches from heat source. Broil duck, basting again with sauce, about 5 minutes, or until skin is crisp and brown and juices run clear when thigh is pierced with a knife.

- To serve, reheat remaining sauce over low heat. Arrange duck quarters on individual serving plates; spoon sauce over. Garnish each serving with thinly slivered orange peel and mint sprig, if desired.

# *Duck Breasts with Raspberry Sauce*

*Seductively simple*

- *½ cup dry red wine*
- *¼ cup soy sauce*
- *¼ cup vegetable oil*
- *¼ teaspoon pepper*
- *4 duck breasts, skinned and boned*

## *Raspberry Sauce*

- *¼ cup seedless black raspberry preserves*
- *¼ cup water*
- *1½ tablespoons Dijon mustard*
- *1 teaspoon lime juice*
- *1 teaspoon soy sauce*
- *½ teaspoon pepper*
- *½ teaspoon steak sauce*
- *¼ teaspoon crushed caraway seeds*
- *⅛ teaspoon salt*

*Serves 4*

- Combine first 4 ingredients, stirring well. Place duck breasts in a shallow dish; pour marinade over meat. Cover and refrigerate for 2 to 2½ hours, turning meat occasionally.

- Combine all sauce ingredients in a small saucepan; cook over low heat until thoroughly warmed.

- Remove duck breasts from marinade, and place on broiler rack; reserve marinade. Broil 5 inches from heat 15 to 20 minutes, turning and basting once. Slice meat. Serve with raspberry sauce.

# *Rock Cornish Hens with Fruited Stuffing*

*A festive meal*

- *1½ cups herb-seasoned stuffing croutons*
- *½ cup drained canned apricot halves, cut in pieces*
- *½ cup quartered seedless green grapes*
- *⅓ cup chopped pecans*
- *¼ cup butter, melted*
- *¾ cup apricot nectar*
- *1 tablespoon chopped fresh parsley*
- *4 Rock Cornish hens (1½ pounds each)*
- *salt and pepper*
- *2 teaspoons soy sauce*

*Serves 4*

- Combine stuffing croutons, apricots, grapes, pecans, butter, 2 tablespoons apricot nectar, parsley, and ¼ teaspoon salt in a bowl; mix lightly. Sprinkle hen cavities with salt and pepper. Fill each with stuffing mixture.
- Bake at 350° for 1½ hours, basting occasionally with remaining apricot nectar combined with soy sauce.

# *Turkey Marsala*

*A twist on a classic*

- *4 turkey breast fillets*
- *4 tablespoons butter*
- *1 clove garlic*
- *4 anchovy fillets, soaked in milk (optional)*
- *capers*
- *4 slices mozzarella cheese*
- *2 teaspoons chopped fresh marjoram*
- *1 tablespoon chopped fresh parsley*
- *3 tablespoons Marsala wine*
- *1/2 cup heavy cream*
- *salt and pepper*

*Serves 4 to 6*

- Flatten turkey breasts between two sheets of wax paper with a meat mallet or rolling pin.
- Melt butter in a sauté pan. When foaming, add garlic and turkey. Cook until lightly browned. Remove from pan.
- Drain anchovy fillets and rinse well. Dry on paper towels. Place a slice of cheese on top of each turkey fillet and arrange anchovies and capers on top. Sprinkle with chopped herbs and return turkey to pan.
- Cook turkey 5 minutes over moderate heat, until turkey is done and cheese has melted. Remove to a serving dish and keep warm. Return pan to heat and add Marsala. Scrape browned pan juices off bottom and reduce heat. Add cream and whisk in well. Lower heat and simmer gently, uncovered, for a few minutes to thicken sauce. Season sauce with salt and pepper and spoon over turkey fillets.

# *Turkey Fillets with Pistachios*

*When entertaining, consider this dish from comedienne extraordinaire — Carol Burnett.*

- *1 cup butter*
- *6 turkey fillets, cut from breast (approximately 6 ounces each)*
- *salt and pepper to taste*
- *4 shallots, finely chopped*
- *4 large fresh mushrooms, sliced*
- *2 tablespoons flour*
- *1/3 cup dry white wine*
- *2/3 cup chicken broth*
- *2 egg yolks*
- *1/2 cup heavy cream*
- *1/3 cup chopped pistachios*
- *1/4 teaspoon tarragon*
- *1 tablespoon lemon juice*

*Serves 6*

- Melt 1/4 cup butter in a large skillet. Sauté turkey on both sides until golden. Season with salt and pepper. Remove from pan and set aside.
- Add shallots to pan and sauté for 5 minutes. Add mushrooms and cook another 5 minutes, adding more butter if needed. Sprinkle in flour and cook about 3 minutes. Add wine and broth, stirring until slightly thickened.
- Return fillets to pan. Cover, and cook 15 minutes on low heat.
- Beat cream and egg yolks together. Add some wine sauce to cream mixture, then stir cream into wine sauce. Stir until thickened. Add pistachios, tarragon, and lemon juice. Season to taste.

# *Marmalade Glazed Turkey Breast*

*Now the secret to Mom's moist turkey breast is out.*

- *½ cup orange marmalade*
- *1 tablespoon soy sauce*
- *1 tablespoon fresh lemon juice*
- *1 tablespoon Dijon mustard*
- *1 tablespoon lemon zest*
- *5 pound turkey breast*
- *2 oranges, peeled and segmented*

*Serves 10 to 12*

- In a small bowl, combine marmalade, soy sauce, lemon juice, mustard, and lemon zest.
- Place turkey breast, skin-side down in a 2-quart microwave-proof rectangular dish. Brush with ½ of marmalade mixture. Microwave on high for 35 minutes. Turn turkey skin-side up; brush with remaining marmalade mixture. Microwave on medium for 40 to 45 minutes, or until juices run clear and meat thermometer reaches 170°. Transfer turkey to a serving platter. Let stand, tented with aluminum foil, for 10 to 15 minutes.
- Skim excess fat from pan juices and discard. Add orange segments to juices in dish. Microwave on high for 2 minutes, or until sauce is hot. Thinly slice turkey and serve with orange sauce.
- To cook in a conventional oven, place breast in a shallow pan. Cover loosely with foil and bake at 325° for 2½ to 3 hours. Baste as desired and prepare orange sauce on stovetop.

# *Turkey Supreme*

*A favorite of one of the Junior League of Binghamton's founding members*

*½ cup butter*
*2 tablespoons flour*
*¾ cup heavy cream*
*¾ cup chopped green pepper*
*2 onions, chopped*
*3 teaspoons minced fresh parsley*
*1 teaspoon sage*
*1 teaspoon salt*
*dash of pepper*
*4 cups cooked turkey, diced*
*¼ cup dry sherry*

*Serves 4*

- Melt 3 tablespoons butter in a skillet. Blend in flour and stir in cream, gradually, until sauce has thickened. Stir in pepper, onions, parsley, sage, salt, and pepper. Stir in turkey. Add 2 tablespoons butter to skillet. Continue cooking over low heat approximately 30 minutes, uncovered, stirring occasionally.
- Transfer to a baking dish. Pour sherry over top, dot with remaining butter, and place under broiler or in hot oven until lightly browned.

# MEATS & MORE

# MEATS & MORE



## *Beef*



## *Pork*



## *Veal*



## *Lamb*



## *Featured Regional Specialties*



## *Condiments*

# *Lobster Stuffed Tenderloin of Beef*

*There simply isn't a finer dish.*

*3-4 pounds whole beef tenderloin*
*2 (4 ounce) lobster tails, cooked*
*1 tablespoon butter, melted*
*1½ teaspoons lemon juice*
*10-12 slices bacon*

## *Sauce*

*½ cup chopped scallions*
*½ cup butter*
*½ cup dry white wine*
*⅛ teaspoon garlic salt*

*Serves 8 to 10*

- To butterfly beef, cut tenderloin lengthwise to within ½ inch of end.
- Remove lobster meat from shells; cut in half, lengthwise. Place lobster end-to-end inside beef.
- Combine 1 tablespoon melted butter with lemon juice and drizzle on lobster. Re-assemble beef tenderloin and tie securely with string at 1-inch intervals.
- Refrigerate for several hours until ready to bake. Before baking, lay bacon strips across width of tenderloin. (When strips are placed properly, finished roast will resemble a large lobster tail.) Place on rack in a shallow pan. Roast at 425° for 40 minutes for rare, 50 minutes for medium, or until done to taste.
- While meat is roasting, sauté scallions in ½ cup butter over low heat until tender. Stir frequently. Add wine and garlic salt. Heat thoroughly.
- Present roasted tenderloin "tail" with sauce as an accompaniment. Slice.

# *Beef Tenderloin with Bordelaise Sauce*

*Add a French accent to any festive occasion.*

- *4 pounds beef tenderloin, trimmed*
- *1 clove garlic, halved*
- *3 tablespoons soy sauce*
- *salt and pepper to taste*
- *2 tablespoons butter*
- *1 clove garlic, minced*
- *1 onion, sliced*
- *sprigs of fresh parsley*
- *1 carrot, sliced*
- *6 peppercorns*
- *1 bay leaf*
- *2 whole cloves*
- *2 tablespoons flour*
- *1 (10 ounce) can beef broth*
- *½ cup Burgundy wine*
- *1 tablespoon finely chopped fresh parsley*

*Serves 10 to 12*

- Rub roast with garlic clove halves. Brush with soy sauce and season with salt and pepper. Roast at 450° for at least 25 minutes, or until done.
- While tenderloin is roasting, prepare sauce. Slowly heat butter in a saucepan. Add next 7 ingredients. Sauté until onion is golden. Remove from heat; add flour. Return to heat, stirring until smooth and flour is lightly browned. Gradually stir in broth over medium heat. Bring to a boil, stirring constantly. Reduce heat, and simmer 10 minutes. (At this point, sauce may be refrigerated until later use.)
- When ready to serve, strain sauce, reserving liquid portion only. Add wine and parsley. Serve sauce alongside roasted tenderloin.

# *London Broil with Hunter's Sauce*

*Moist and savory, perfect for the hearty appetite*

*2 pounds London Broil*
*2 tablespoons peanut, vegetable, or corn oil*
*salt and pepper to taste*
*3 tablespoons butter*

## *Hunter's Sauce*

*1/3 pound fresh mushrooms, sliced (about 2 cups)*
*1 tablespoon finely chopped shallots*
*1 tablespoon butter*
*salt and pepper to taste*
*1/3 cup dry red wine*
*1/2 cup peeled, chopped tomatoes*
*1/2 cup beef broth*
*1/2 teaspoon chopped fresh tarragon (or 1/4 teaspoon dried)*
*1 teaspoon cornstarch*

*Serves 6*

- Rub steak on both sides with oil and sprinkle with salt and pepper. Use a generous amount of pepper.
- Broil or grill meat 4 to 5 inches from source of heat for 3 to 5 minutes on each side. Cooking time will depend on desired degree of doneness.
- Transfer steak to a hot platter and dot with butter. Let steak stand in a warm place about 5 minutes to redistribute the internal juices of the meat. Juices will accumulate as steak stands. Add these to Hunter's sauce.
- To prepare Hunter's sauce, sauté mushrooms and shallots in butter in a saucepan. Add salt and pepper to taste. Cook about 10 minutes. Add wine and simmer, briefly. Add tomatoes, beef broth, reserved juices, and tarragon. Cook about 5 minutes, stirring occasionally. Blend cornstarch and a small amount of water. Stir into sauce. Cook briefly and serve with steak.

# *Marinated Beef Roast*

*Tempting and tender*

- *3-4 pounds beef eye round roast*
- *1/3 cup soy sauce*
- *1/3 cup dry sherry*
- *1/3 cup lime juice*
- *2 tablespoons vegetable oil*
- *1 tablespoon minced fresh ginger root*
- *1 tablespoon honey*
- *2 cloves garlic, minced*

- Combine soy sauce, sherry, lime juice, oil, ginger, honey, and garlic. Place roast in a non-metal dish or plastic bag; add marinade, turning to coat. Cover dish or tie bag securely and marinate in refrigerator 6 to 8 hours (or overnight, if desired), turning occasionally.
- Remove roast from marinade, reserving liquid. Place on rack in open roasting pan. Insert meat thermometer so that bulb is centered in thickest part of roast. Do not add water. Do not cover. Roast at 325° until thermometer registers 135°. Allow 20 to 22 minutes per pound. Brush roast with reserved marinade during the last 20 minutes of cooking. Carve into thin slices.

# *Prime Rib Roast with Mustard Crumb Crust*

*Why not rekindle the tradition of the family Sunday dinner with this roast?*

- 8 *pounds prime rib beef roast, 3-4 ribs, fat trimmed to ½-inch thickness*
- 8 *slices firm-textured white bread, roughly crumbled*
- ½ *cup chopped fresh parsley*
- ⅓ *cup Dijon mustard*
- ⅓ *cup mayonnaise*
- ¼ *cup grated Parmesan cheese*
- 2 *tablespoons lemon juice*
- 2 *cloves garlic, crushed*
- ½ *teaspoon salt*
- ½ *teaspoon thyme*
- ½ *teaspoon basil*
- ¼ *teaspoon pepper*

*Serves 8 to 10*

- Heat oven to 350°. Place beef, fat-side up, on rack in a large open roasting pan. Insert thermometer into center of roast, making sure tip doesn't touch bone. Roast meat about 1½ hours, or until thermometer registers 120°.

- In a medium bowl, combine bread, parsley, mustard, mayonnaise, Parmesan cheese, lemon juice, garlic, salt, thyme, basil, and pepper; stir until well blended.

- Remove roast from oven, maintaining oven temperature. Pat bread mixture evenly over top. Return to oven; roast 20 to 30 minutes longer, or until crust is browned and thermometer registers 130°. Remove roast from pan to a serving platter, reserving drippings in pan. Let roast stand for 30 to 40 minutes before serving.

# *Sauerbraten*

*Here is an 80-year-old recipe that's still drawing rave reviews.*

- 3-5 *pounds boneless beef ("pot") roast*
- 2 *cups vinegar*
- 1 *onion, sliced*
- ½ *teaspoon salt*
- ¼ *teaspoon pepper*
- 1 *cup ketchup*
- 2 *cups water*
- 2 *tablespoons sugar*
- 2 *bay leaves*
- 12 *gingersnaps, crushed*
- 3 *tablespoons sherry*

*Serves 8 or more*

- Combine beef roast, vinegar, onion, salt, and pepper in a non-metal container. Marinate, refrigerated, for 72 hours, turning at least once each day.
- Remove roast from marinade, reserving one cup of liquid and sliced onion. Place roast, onion, reserved marinade, ketchup, water, sugar, and bay leaves in a pot. Cook over medium-low heat for 1½ to 2 hours, or until tender.
- Remove meat from pot. Add gingersnaps to remaining liquid. Heat gently until gravy has thickened. Add sherry.
- Strain gravy before serving alongside sliced roast.

*Serve with noodles and red cabbage for a meal "just like mother used to make."*

# *Congressional Beef with Onion Sauce*

*It's hats off to our Congressman Matt McHugh for providing us with this recipe.*

- *4-6 pounds beef brisket*
- *1 onion, quartered*
- *1 carrot, peeled and diced*
- *1 stalk celery, diced*
- *2 teaspoons salt*
- *6 peppercorns*
- *6 whole cloves*
- *2 bay leaves*
- *water*
- *1 egg, lightly beaten*
- *½ cup dry bread crumbs*

## *Onion Sauce*

- *2 tablespoons sugar*
- *1 tablespoon reserved fat*
- *2 medium onions, sliced*
- *1 tablespoon flour*
- *1 cup reserved meat broth*
- *1 teaspoon white vinegar*
- *½ teaspoon salt*

*Serves 8 to 10*

- Trim excess fat from brisket and render in a Dutch oven over medium-high heat until 2 tablespoons of melted fat have accumulated. Remove fatty pieces and discard. (If there is not enough fat on brisket, use a strip of bacon.) Brown brisket in hot fat until meat is nicely seared on all sides. Pour off fat, reserving 1 tablespoon. Add vegetables and seasonings. Cover with water and simmer, covered, over medium heat for 2 to 3 hours, or until meat is tender, but not falling apart.

- Remove meat from broth, reserving 1 cup, and place in a shallow casserole or baking dish. Brush beaten egg on all sides of meat. Sprinkle with bread crumbs and brown in a 350° oven.

- To prepare onion sauce, brown sugar in reserved fat. Add sliced onions and simmer until tender. Add flour and brown lightly before adding broth, vinegar, and salt. Cook and stir until smooth.

- Slice meat thinly across the grain and serve with onion sauce.

# *Steak au Poivre*

*Here's a recipe that's sure to make you feel as if you're dining out in your own home.*

- 3 *tablespoons peppercorns*
- 4 *½-pound boneless shell steaks, ¾-inch thick*
- 1½ *tablespoons vegetable oil*
- 1½ *tablespoons butter*
- ¼ *cup minced shallots*
- ½ *cup cognac*
- 1 *cup beef broth*
- ⅔ *cup heavy cream*
- *watercress sprigs for garnish*

*Serves 4*

- Using the bottom of a heavy skillet, crush peppercorns between 2 sheets of wax paper. Press pepper into both sides of steaks. Cover steaks loosely with wax paper and let stand at room temperature for 1 hour.
- In a large heavy skillet, heat oil and butter over medium-high heat until foam subsides. Sauté steaks for 2 to 2½ minutes on each side. Transfer steaks to a platter and keep warm; cover loosely.
- Pour off almost all remaining fat in skillet. Add shallots, and cook over medium heat, stirring, until softened. Add cognac and boil until reduced by half. Add broth; reduce again. Add cream and simmer mixture, stirring occasionally, until slightly thickened. Season sauce with salt, if desired, and pour into a heated sauceboat.
- Garnish steaks with watercress and serve sauce separately.

# *Sesame Beef*

*An authentic Korean barbecue*

- *2 pounds London broil*
- *1 tablespoon sesame seeds*
- *3 scallions, finely chopped*
- *4 cloves garlic, finely minced*
- *1/4 cup soy sauce*
- *2 tablespoons beef stock*
- *black and cayenne pepper to taste*
- *crushed red pepper to taste*

*Serves 8 to 10*

- Cut steak diagonally across the grain into very thin slices. Meat will slice more easily if it has been placed in the freezer for 20 minutes.
- Place sesame seeds in a pan and brown over low heat. Grind seeds.
- Combine ground sesame seeds with remaining ingredients. Place in a large bowl or pan and coat sliced beef; marinate at least 1 hour.
- Beef can be cooked over charcoal, open electric grill, or under broiler. Cooking time should be brief, only 30 seconds on each side.

# *Beef Burgundy*

*The aroma from this simmering stew will fill your home.*

¼ *pound bacon, chopped*
3 *pounds sirloin tip (or chuck), cut into 1-inch cubes*
4 *onions, chopped*
1 *pound fresh mushrooms, sliced*
⅓ *cup flour*
1 *beef bouillon cube*
2 *cups red wine (preferably Burgundy)*
½ *teaspoon thyme*
½ *teaspoon marjoram*
1 *teaspoon salt*
½ *teaspoon pepper*
1 *bay leaf*
¼ *teaspoon cloves*
⅛ *teaspoon nutmeg*
3 *tablespoons brandy*

*Serves 6 to 8*

- Fry bacon; remove from skillet. Brown meat in hot fat until almost black.
- Add mushrooms and onion; sauté briefly. Stir in flour; mix well. Gradually add bouillon and wine, stirring constantly until thickened. Add seasonings. Cover and simmer, very gently, for 1½ hours (2½ hours with chuck).
- Remove cover; stir well. Cook an additional 15 minutes uncovered. Sauce should be dark and thick. If necessary, add 1 teaspoon cornstarch mixed with a little water to thicken.
- Warm brandy; ignite and pour over beef.

*This recipe can be prepared in a crock pot.*

# *Beer Hall Beef Stew*

*Hail, hail, the gang's all here.*

- *2 tablespoons vegetable oil*
- *1½ pounds beef round steak, trimmed and cubed*
- *1 large onion, chopped*
- *10 ounces fresh mushrooms, thickly sliced*
- *12 ounces dark beer, ale, or non-alcoholic beer*
- *1¼ cups beef broth*
- *2 tablespoons chopped fresh parsley*
- *1 clove garlic, crushed*
- *1 bay leaf*
- *¼ teaspoon thyme*
- *¼ teaspoon cloves*
- *¼ teaspoon pepper*
- *1 teaspoon flour*
- *1 tablespoon cider vinegar*
- *½ teaspoon sugar*

*Serves 6*

- Add oil, beef, onion, and mushrooms to a 4-quart saucepan; partially cover pan with lid. Cook beef and vegetables over medium heat 5 to 6 minutes, or until vegetables are softened.
- Stir in beer, 1 cup beef broth, parsley, garlic, bay leaf, thyme, cloves, and pepper. Bring to a boil; reduce heat to low. Simmer, partially covered, 1 hour, or until meat is tender.
- In a small bowl, stir remaining ¼ cup beef broth into flour until smooth; add to saucepan. Simmer 5 minutes longer, stirring occasionally, until liquid is slightly thickened; remove from heat. Stir in vinegar and sugar. Remove bay leaf and serve.

# *Marinated Beef*

*These marvelous variations turn many cuts of beef into flavorful dinner offerings.*

## *Fabulous Teriyaki*

- 1 *cup firmly packed brown sugar*
- 2 *cups water*
- 1½ *cups soy sauce*
- 1 *clove garlic, sliced*
- 1 *tablespoon ginger*

• Make syrup of sugar and water; boil. Add remaining ingredients; simmer 1 hour. Marinate meat at least 3 hours.

*Try this with a London Broil. Marinate beef and grill it ahead of time. Slice and serve at room temperature.*

## *Hula Baste*

- ½ *cup firmly packed brown sugar*
- ½ *cup wine vinegar*
- ½ *cup pineapple juice*
- 2 *teaspoons salt*
- ½ *teaspoon garlic powder*
- 1 *cup soy sauce*

• Mix all ingredients and bring to a boil. Marinate meat at least 4 hours.

*Wonderful on kabobs. Be sure to add fresh pineapple to your choice of vegetables.*

## *Greek Marinade*

- 1 *cup olive oil*
- ⅓ *cup lemon juice*
- 2 *cloves garlic, minced*
- 2 *tablespoons oregano*

• Mix all ingredients and bring to a boil. Marinate meat at least 4 hours.

*Wonderful on any cut of beef, but our favorite is filet mignon.*

# *First Lady Chili*

*A little bit of Texas from Lady Bird Johnson, former First Lady.*

- *4 pounds chili meat*
- *1 large onion, chopped*
- *2 cloves garlic, minced*
- *1 teaspoon oregano*
- *1 teaspoon cumin*
- *6 teaspoons chili powder, or to taste*
- *1½ cups canned whole tomatoes*
- *2-6 generous dashes bottled hot pepper sauce*
- *salt to taste*
- *2 cups hot water*

## *Enchilada Fixings*

- *1 onion, finely chopped*
- *3 cups grated cheese (cheddar, Monterey Jack, or American)*
- *12 corn tortillas*

*Serves 8 to 10*

- To make chili, place meat, onion, and garlic in a large, heavy frying pan or Dutch oven. Cook until meat is light in color. Add oregano, cumin, chili powder, tomatoes, hot pepper sauce, salt, and hot water. Bring to a boil; lower heat, and simmer about 1 hour. Skim off fat during cooking.
- To make enchiladas, place tortillas, one at a time, in a pot of boiling water for one second.
- Place ¼ teaspoon onion, 1 tablespoon chili, and 1 tablespoon cheese on each tortilla; fold over or roll. Place filled tortillas side by side in a glass baking dish. Pour about 1 cup of chili liquid over enchiladas.
- Bake 10 to 12 minutes in a 350° oven before sprinkling with 1½ cups cheese. Return to oven for 5 more minutes. Serve immediately.

## *Sloppy Beef*

*Surprise your troops with this all-time kids' favorite.*
*It's so easy, you can even let them prepare it.*

- *1 pound ground beef*
- *12 ounces chili sauce*
- *2 tablespoons brown sugar*
- *1 tablespoon vinegar*
- *1 large onion, chopped*
- *salt and pepper*

- Brown ground beef in a frying pan. Drain fat. Add remaining ingredients. Simmer 1 to 1½ hours. Spoon over toasted buns.

*Serves 4*

## *Hot Dog Sauce*

*There is nothing like an old-fashioned hot dog with all the fixin's to remind you of happy afternoons spent at county fairs, ball games, or even on the boardwalk!*

- *2 pounds ground beef*
- *1½ cups diced onion*
- *14 ounces ketchup*
- *2 tablespoons salt*
- *1½ ounces paprika*
- *1 ounce chili powder*
- *1 tablespoon nutmeg*
- *1 tablespoon pepper*
- *1 tabespoon sugar*
- *1 teaspoon cloves*
- *6 cup water*
- *1 cup flour*

- Brown ground beef in a frying pan. Drain fat.
- Place ground beef, onion, ketchup, and seasonings in a large roasting pan. Add 5 cups water. Mix remaining cup water with flour. Add to roasting pan. Stir.
- Bake at 325° for 2 hours, stirring occasionally. Serve over grilled hot dogs on toasted buns.

# *Barbecued Pork on a Bun*

*Great for a casual get-together*

- *2 tablespoons vegetable oil*
- *3 green peppers, chopped*
- *2 large onions, chopped*
- *1/4 cup chili powder*
- *3 pounds pork cubes*
- *6 ounces tomato paste*
- *1/2 cup cider vinegar*
- *1/2 cup firmly packed brown sugar*
- *2 tablespoons prepared mustard*
- *1 tablespoon Worcestershire sauce*
- *2 teaspoons salt*
- *1 cup water*
- *sandwich buns*

*Serves 6 to 8*

- In a 5-quart Dutch oven, cook green peppers and onions in oil until tender and lightly browned. Stir in chili powder; cook 1 minute.
- Add pork cubes, tomato paste, vinegar, brown sugar, mustard, Worcestershire sauce, salt, and water. Heat to boiling; reduce heat to low. Cover and simmer 2½ to 3 hours, stirring often, until meat falls apart when tested with a fork. Skim fat from meat mixture.
- With 2 forks, pull meat into shreds. Serve hot, or cover and refrigerate to reheat later. Serve barbecued pork on toasted sandwich buns.

# *Spiedies*

*Broome County is home to the original "spiedie." These regional specialties are essentially chunks of meat marinated for days before being skewered and grilled. Fantastically tender bitefuls of pure flavor result. Herewith, some local favorites:*

## *Blue Ribbon Chicken Spiedies*

- *3½ pounds boneless chicken breast, cut into chunks*
- *2 cups olive oil*
- *5 tablespoons balsamic vinegar*
- *2 tablespoons light beer*
- *2 tablespoons grated Romano cheese*
- *2 tablespoons parsley*
- *2 teaspoons salt*
- *1 teaspoon garlic powder*
- *1 teaspoon minced onion*
- *1 teaspoon pepper*
- *1 teaspoon oregano*

- Combine all marinade ingredients. Add chicken and marinate at least 24 hours (preferably 48), turning occasionally.
- Skewer and grill chicken, basting with marinade.

## *Grand Prize Chicken Spiedies*

- *2-3 pounds boneless chicken breast, cut into chunks*
- *1 cup vegetable oil*
- *½ cup lemonade*
- *10 crushed peppercorns*
- *2 cloves garlic, crushed*
- *2 teaspoons ginger*
- *2 teaspoons curry powder*
- *2 teaspoons dry mustard*
- *2 teaspoons rosemary*

- Combine all marinade ingredients. Add chicken and marinate at least 24 hours (preferably 48), turning occasionally.
- Skewer and grill chicken, basting with marinade.

*Swordfish can be substituted for chicken.*

# *And More Spiedies*

*Spiedies are traditionally served in a slice of Italian bread.*

## *"The Original" Lamb Spiedies*

*3 pounds cubed lamb*
*1 cup olive oil*
*1/2 cup lemon juice*
*1/2 cup dry wine*
*5 cloves garlic, minced*
*2 teaspoons celery salt*
*2 tablespoons each chopped fresh basil, mint, oregano, rosemary, and parsley*

- Combine all marinade ingredients. Add meat and marinate 72 hours, turning occasionally.
- Skewer and grill meat, basting with marinade.

## *Award Winning Beef Spiedies*

*4 pounds cubed beef*
*1 cup olive oil*
*1 cup cider vinegar*
*2/3 cup lime juice*
*1/2 cup margarine, melted*
*3 tablespoons Worcestershire sauce*
*3 teaspoons salt*
*1 teaspoon white pepper*
*1/2 teaspoon cayenne pepper*
*1 clove garlic, minced*
*1 teaspoon dried mint*

- Combine all marinade ingredients. Add meat and marinate 72 hours, turning occasionally.
- Skewer and grill meat, basting with marinade.

## *Peppy Pork Spiedies*

*4 pounds cubed pork*
*3 cups vegetable oil*
*1/4 cup wine*
*1/2 pound pepperoni, diced*
*juice from 2 lemons*
*2 tablespoons prepared mustard*
*4 cloves garlic, minced*
*2 bay leaves*
*salt and pepper*

- Combine all marinade ingredients. Add meat and marinate 72 hours, turning occasionally.
- Skewer and grill meat, basting with marinade.

# *Bleu Cheese Stuffed Chops*

*An intriguing combination of textures and flavors*

- *4 pork loin rib chops, each 1½-inches thick*
- *½ cup shredded carrot*
- *¼ cup chopped pecans*
- *¼ cup crumbled bleu cheese*
- *1 scallion, thinly sliced*
- *1 teaspoon Worcestershire sauce*

## *Creamy Sauce*

- *4 teaspoons flour*
- *¼ cup plain yogurt*
- *¾ cup milk*
- *½ teaspoon instant chicken bouillon granules*
- *dash of pepper*

*Serves 4*

- In a small bowl, combine carrot, pecans, bleu cheese, scallion, and Worcestershire sauce.
- Trim excess fat from pork chops. Cut a pocket in each chop from fat side almost to bone. Spoon ¼ cup of cheese stuffing into each pocket; close with toothpicks.
- Bake chops at 350° for 40 to 50 minutes. (Chops can also be grilled over a drip pan on a medium-hot covered grill for 40 minutes, or until no pink remains.)
- To prepare creamy sauce, in a small saucepan, stir flour into yogurt. Add milk, bouillon granules, and pepper. Cook, stirring frequently, until thick and bubbly. Cook and stir 1 minute more.
- Serve chops topped with sauce. Sprinkle with additional bleu cheese, if desired.

# *Zesty Pork Kabobs*

*The fresh corn makes this one of our summer favorites.*

- *1 pound boneless pork loin, cut into 1½-inch cubes*
- *1 cup margarita mix (or 1 cup lime juice, 4 teaspoons sugar, ½ teaspoon salt)*
- *1 teaspoon coriander*
- *1 clove garlic, minced*
- *2 tablespoons butter, softened*
- *2 teaspoons lime juice*
- *⅛ teaspoon sugar*
- *1 tablespoon minced fresh parsley*
- *1 large green or red pepper, cut into 1-inch chunks*
- *2 ears corn, cut into 8 pieces*

*Serves 4 to 6*

- Combine margarita mix, coriander, and garlic. Marinate pork cubes for at least 30 minutes.
- Blend butter, lime juice, sugar, and parsley; set aside.
- Thread pork cubes onto skewers, alternating with corn and pepper. (Bamboo skewers should be soaked in water for 20 to 30 minutes before using.) Grill over hot coals, basting with butter mixture, 8 to 10 minutes, turning frequently.

# *Fantastic Pork Fajitas*

*Olé!*

- 1 *pound lean, boneless pork*
- 2 *cloves garlic, minced*
- 1 *teaspoon oregano*
- ½ *teaspoon cumin*
- 1 *teaspoon seasoned salt*
- 2 *tablespoons orange juice*
- 2 *tablespoons vinegar*
- *dash of bottled hot pepper sauce*
- 1 *tablespoon vegetable oil*
- 1 *onion, sliced*
- 1 *green pepper, sliced*
- 4 *flour tortillas*
- *scallion tops, sliced*
- *shredded lettuce*
- *bottled salsa*

*Serves 4*

- Slice pork across the grain into ⅛-inch strips. Marinate pork strips in garlic, oregano, cumin, salt, orange juice, vinegar, and hot pepper sauce for 10 minutes.
- Heat a heavy skillet or griddle until hot (if using electric skillet, set at 400°). Add oil, onion, green pepper, and pork strips; stir-fry until pork is no longer pink, about 3 to 5 minutes.
- Serve pork with flour tortillas and accompany with sliced scallions, shredded lettuce, and salsa.

## *Father's Day Grilled Pork Tenderloin*

*Just the thing to celebrate the important people in your life.*

- 3 *pounds pork tenderloin, cut into ¾-inch thick medallions*
- 1 *cup chicken broth*
- ¼ *cup soy sauce*
- ¼ *cup honey*
- 2 *tablespoons sherry*
- 1 *tablespoon lemon juice*
- 1 *clove garlic, minced*
- 1 *teaspoon cinnamon*
- 1 *teaspoon salt*
- 1 *tablespoon grated fresh ginger root*

*Serves 6 to 8*

- Marinate pork in a mixture of all remaining ingredients for at least 2 hours. Grill over hot coals, turning and basting often with marinade.

## *Orange Pork Tenderloin*

*Tangy and tender!*

- 2 *pork tenderloins*
- 1 *tablespoon butter, softened*
- ¼ *teaspoon thyme*
- *dash cayenne pepper*
- ¾ *cup orange juice*
- 1 *tablespoon flour*
- 1½ *teaspoons sugar*
- 1 *teaspoon aromatic bitters*

*Serves 4 to 6*

- Mix butter, thyme, and cayenne pepper. Spread evenly over pork. Place tenderloins in a shallow roasting pan and pour orange juice over meat. Roast in a 375° oven for 25 to 30 minutes.
- Remove tenderloins to a serving platter; keep warm. Measure basting liquid into a small saucepan, adding additional orange juice, if necessary, to make ¾ cup. Quickly whisk in flour, sugar, and bitters. Cook and stir until mixture boils and thickens. Cut tenderloins into 1-inch slices and serve with sauce.

## *Pork Chops Julienne*

*We've added a creative touch to this back to basics recipe.*

- *4 pork chops*
- *1 tablespoon vegetable oil*
- *2 cups chicken broth*
- *1/4 teaspoon salt*
- *1/8 teaspoon pepper*
- *4 celery stalks, julienned*
- *4 large carrots, julienned*
- *1 tablespoon flour*

*Serves 4*

- Brown pork chops in oil.
- Add broth and cover chops with vegetables. Simmer 30 to 40 minutes.
- Remove chops and vegetables from pan. Whisk flour into broth to make gravy.

## *Lemon and Herb Loin of Pork*

*A versatile entrée for family or company*

- *5-6 pounds boneless pork loin*
- *1/2 cup chopped fresh parsley*
- *1/3 cup chopped onion*
- *1/4 cup lemon zest*
- *1 tablespoon basil*
- *3 cloves garlic, crushed*
- *1/2 cup olive oil*
- *3/4 cup dry sherry*

*Serves 10 to 12*

- Score pork with a sharp knife. Combine parsley, onion, lemon zest, basil, and garlic in a bowl. Whisk in oil. Rub into pork. Wrap in foil and refrigerate overnight.
- Let pork stand at room temperature 1 hour before roasting. Set on rack in a shallow pan. Roast until meat thermometer registers 170°, or about 2½ hours. Set meat aside. Skim grease from juice; add sherry to juice and cook over low heat 2 minutes. Spoon gravy over roast.

# *Spareribs*

*Be sure to have plenty of napkins on hand.*

- *1½ cups ketchup*
- *1 cup whiskey*
- *¾ cup chili sauce*
- *⅓ cup Worcestershire sauce*
- *⅓ cup brown sugar*
- *3 tablespoons lemon juice*
- *1 tablespoon paprika*
- *1 teaspoon salt*
- *1 garlic clove, crushed*
- *¼ teaspoon hot pepper sauce*
- *5 pounds pork back ribs*
- *salt and pepper*
- *thin slices of onion*
- *thin slices of lemon*

*Serves 6 to 8*

- Combine first 10 ingredients in large saucepan. Heat to boiling. Reduce heat. Simmer 30 to 45 minutes, or until sauce is slightly thickened.
- Cut meat into 3 to 4 rib portions. Season with salt and pepper. Put on rack in shallow baking pan. Bake at 375° for 30 minutes. Remove from rack. Drain off fat. Return ribs to baking pan, meaty-side down. Brush with sauce.
- Reduce heat to 300°. Bake 30 minutes; turn ribs and brush with sauce. Top each rib with an onion slice. Bake 1 hour, brushing with remaining sauce until ribs are tender and brown. Add lemon slices to ribs during last ½ hour of baking.

# *Crown Roast of Pork*

*A royal offering*

- *1 crown roast of pork (about 7 pounds)*
- *1 tablespoon chopped fresh thyme (or 1 teaspoon dried)*
- *½ teaspoon salt*

## *Stuffing*

- *1 cup diced leeks*
- *1 cup diced celery*
- *2 tablespoons chopped fresh thyme (or 2 teaspoons dried)*
- *½ cup unsalted butter*
- *20 small white onions, peeled*
- *7 cups cubed brioche*
- *1 cup dried pitted prunes*
- *½ cup dried apricots*
- *½ cup golden raisins*
- *1½ cups chicken broth*
- *¼ cup chopped fresh parsley*
- *½ teaspoon pepper*
- *¼ teaspoon salt*

*Serves 8 to 10*

- Sauté leeks, celery, and thyme in ¼ cup butter until softened, about 7 minutes. Remove vegetables to a large bowl.
- Sauté onions in remaining butter until lightly browned, about 5 minutes. Add to leek mixture along with brioche, prunes, apricots, raisins, broth, parsley, pepper, and salt.
- To prepare meat, combine thyme and salt. Rub salt mixture over roast. Spoon half the stuffing into center of roast. Spoon remaining stuffing into an 8x8x2-inch pan; cover with foil. Place pork in a foil-lined roasting pan, covering stuffing and ends of bones with foil to prevent burning.
- Roast pork at 375° for 2½ to 3 hours, or until meat thermometer registers 160°. Bake extra stuffing with roast for last 45 minutes. Let roast stand 15 minutes before serving.

# *Veal Forestier*

*This distinctive dish is sure to entice.*

- *1 pound veal cutlets, each 1/4-inch thick*
- *1/4 cup flour*
- *1/4 cup butter*
- *1/2 pound fresh mushrooms, sliced*
- *1/2 cup dry vermouth*
- *2 tablespoons water*
- *3/4 teaspoon salt*
- *dash of pepper*
- *1 tablespoon chopped fresh parsley*
- *sautéed cherry tomatoes*
- *parsley sprigs for garnish*

*Serves 4*

- Pound veal cutlets to 1/8-inch thickness. Cut veal into 3x2-inch pieces and coat lightly with flour.
- In a 10-inch skillet over medium-high heat, cook meat in butter, a few pieces at a time, removing pieces as they brown and adding more butter if necessary.
- Add mushrooms, vermouth, water, salt, and pepper to skillet; heat to boiling. Reduce heat to low; cover and simmer 5 minutes, or until mushrooms are tender. Return meat to skillet; heat through. Stir in chopped parsley. Arrange meat on a platter with sautéed cherry tomatoes. Garnish with parsley sprigs.

# *Empire State Veal*

*Governor and Mrs. Cuomo's heritage shines through in this delicious recipe.*

- 1 *pound veal, cut into 3-inch squares*
- 32 *ounces crushed tomatoes*
- 2 *cups bread crumbs*
- ½ *cup grated Locatelli or Parmesan cheese*
- 6 *sprigs parsley, chopped*
- 1½ *cups corn oil*
- ¼ *pound Fontina cheese, diced*
- 2 *medium onions, sliced*
- 12 *bay leaves*

*Serves 4*

- Marinate veal in crushed tomatoes for 2 to 24 hours.
- Combine bread crumbs, Locatelli or Parmesan cheese, and chopped parsley. Place 1 cup oil in skillet and toast bread crumb mixture until golden. Set aside.
- Pour remaining oil into bottom of a 13x9-inch pan, coating entire pan. Dredge veal in bread crumb mixture and place 1 piece of Fontina cheese in center of each square. Overlap sides of veal over cheese. Place each bundle in a baking dish with one onion slice and one bay leaf. Spread remaining crushed tomatoes over the top.
- Bake at 375° for 30 minutes.

# *Veal in Velvet Cream*

*Satiny smooth!*

*4 veal scallops, each ¼-inch thick*
*3 tablespoons butter*
*1 tablespoon olive oil*
*1 cup fresh mushrooms, minced*
*2 tablespoons minced shallots*
*½ cup dry white wine*
*1 cup heavy cream*
*salt and pepper*

*Serves 2*

- Sprinkle veal scallops with salt and pepper. Cut into ¼x2-inch strips. In a skillet, sauté veal in 1 tablespoon butter and 1 tablespoon olive oil for one minute, or until golden.
- Transfer veal with a slotted spoon to a heated dish. Keep covered. Pour pan juices into a bowl.
- Add 2 tablespoons butter to skillet; sauté mushrooms until golden. Add shallots and sauté 1 minute more. Remove pan from heat. Add wine. Return pan to high heat and bring to a boil. Stir in brown bits clinging to bottom and sides of pan. Continue cooking until liquid is reduced to 2 tablespoons. Reduce heat to medium-high. Add pan juices and 1 cup heavy cream, ¼ cup at a time, stirring constantly and reducing each addition for 3 minutes before adding the next. Continue to cook sauce until thickened. Add veal and simmer for 2 minutes, or until hot. Serve immediately.

# *Veal with Lemon Sauce*

*Just right when eating light*

- 8 *veal scallops*
- 3 *tablespoons clarified butter*
- *salt and pepper*
- 1 *tablespoon minced shallots*
- 2 *teaspoons flour*
- ½ *cup chicken stock*
- *juice from ½ lemon*
- *lemon slices and sprigs of parsley for garnish*

*Serves 4*

- Flatten veal scallops between sheets of wax paper. Sauté, 4 at a time, in 2 tablespoons of clarified butter for 1 minute on each side. Sprinkle with salt and pepper and remove from skillet to a warm platter.
- Add one tablespoon clarified butter to pan and sauté shallots. Add flour and cook for 3 minutes, stirring constantly. Add heated chicken stock and simmer until sauce is thickened. Season with lemon juice; salt and pepper to taste.
- Pour sauce over veal. Garnish with thin lemon slices and sprigs of parsley.

# *Veal Chops à l'Arugula*

*A spectacular presentation*

## *The Salad*

- *12 large bunches arugula*
- *1 large tomato, cored*
- *1 red onion, finely chopped*
- *2 tablespoons lemon juice*
- *3 tablespoons balsamic vinegar*
- *5 tablespoons olive oil*
- *1/4 teaspoon salt*
- *1/4 teaspoon white pepper*

## *The Veal*

- *4 veal rib chops*
- *1 1/2 cups bread crumbs*
- *1/3 cup grated Parmesan cheese*
- *1/8 teaspoon nutmeg*
- *1 1/2 teaspoons white pepper*
- *2 eggs*
- *1/2 cup clarified butter*

*Serves 4*

- *The Salad* — Remove and discard arugula stems and cut leaves crosswise into ½-inch pieces; place in a bowl. Dice tomato into ½-inch pieces; add to bowl with arugula. Add onion. Whisk together remaining ingredients; adjust seasoning. Toss salad with dressing just before placing on veal chops.

- *The Veal* — Mix bread crumbs with Parmesan cheese, nutmeg, and pepper; spread in a flat dish. Put eggs in a separate flat dish and beat lightly. Using bones as a handle, dip meat of each chop into egg, then press each side into bread crumbs, turning chops over and over in crumbs until thoroughly coated.

- Transfer chops to waxed paper. With flat side of cleaver, pound on one side very gently to press in crumbs.

- Heat clarified butter in a large skillet. Add chops and sauté until browned on both sides. Transfer cooked chops to a paper towel-lined baking sheet; keep warm in a 250° oven (do not cover chops).

- Transfer each chop to a warm dinner plate and top with a heaping cup of salad.

*Boneless chicken fillets can be used instead of veal.*

# *Medallions of Lamb with Creamy Browned Potatoes*

*Something out of the ordinary*

- 2 *large ripe tomatoes, seeded and diced*
- ½ *red bell pepper, seeded and chopped*
- 1 *small jalapeno pepper, seeded and chopped*
- 1 *teaspoon lime juice*
- *olive oil*
- *salt and freshly ground black pepper*
- 2 *potatoes, boiled, peeled, and cubed*
- ¼ *cup vegetable oil*
- 2 *tablespoons butter*
- ½ *cup heavy cream*
- 1 *boneless loin of lamb, trimmed*
- 4 *tablespoons chopped fresh herbs (parsley, basil, tarragon)*

*Serves 6 to 8*

- In a small bowl, combine tomatoes, peppers, lime juice, 1 teaspoon olive oil, and a generous amount of freshly ground black pepper. Set aside.
- Sauté cubed potatoes in olive oil until golden. Drain off oil; add butter and heavy cream. Season with salt and pepper. Simmer until cream begins to thicken. Set aside and keep warm.
- Season lamb medallions with a little olive oil, salt, and pepper. Grill over a hot charcoal or gas grill 3 to 4 minutes per side for medium rare. Arrange plates with lamb, prepared potatoes, and spicy tomatoes. Sprinkle with fresh herbs and serve.

# *Rack of Lamb*

*For your most special friends*

- 2 *racks of lamb, trimmed*
- 1/4 *cup Dijon mustard*
- 1/2 *teaspoon basil*
- 1/4 *teaspoon rosemary*
- 2 *tablespoons olive oil*
- 1 *shallot, minced*
- 1 *clove garlic, minced*
- 1/4 *cup bread crumbs*
- 2 *tablespoons chopped parsley or other fresh herbs to taste*

*Serves 4*

- Mix mustard, basil, rosemary, and olive oil. Brush lamb with marinade. Let marinate several hours.
- Sauté shallot in butter and add garlic, bread crumbs, and parsley. Cook gently.
- Roast lamb at 400° for 20 minutes. Remove from oven. Top lamb with crumb mixture and broil until crispy. Slice chops apart and serve immediately.

# *Butterflied Leg of Lamb*

*A best bet in spring*

- 1 *large leg of lamb, butterfly cut*
- 2 *cups dry vermouth*
- 1/2 *cup vegetable oil*
- 2 *tablespoons tarragon vinegar*
- 1/3 *cup finely chopped onion*
- 1 *tablespoon finely chopped fresh parsley*
- 1 *teaspoon basil*
- 1 *clove garlic, minced*
- 1 *teaspoon Worcestershire sauce*
- 1 *bay leaf, crumbled*
- 1/2 *teaspoon pepper*
- 1 *lemon, thinly sliced*

*Serves 6*

- Combine all ingredients except lamb. Pour into a large shallow dish or roasting pan. Add meat to marinade. Marinate in refrigerator a day or two, turning occasionally.
- Grill lamb, basting frequently with marinade, for 12 to 15 minutes on each side. If oven-broiled, cook for approximately the same amount of time. Spoon heated marinade over meat and serve.

*This is especially good with wild rice and sliced tomatoes.*

# *Minted Lamb Chops with Cucumbers*

*Refreshing and cool—a summertime delight*

- *1 English cucumber (or 2 large stalks celery)*
- *1 tablespoon olive oil*
- *1/2 teaspoon salt*
- *1/8 teaspoon pepper*
- *8 rib lamb chops*
- *1/2 cup red wine*
- *2 tablespoons chopped fresh mint*
- *2 tablespoons butter*

*Serves 4*

- Peel strips of skin from cucumbers about 1/4-inch apart. Halve lengthwise, scoop out seeds, and slice into crescents.
- Heat oil in a frying pan over medium-high heat. Add cucumber, salt, and pepper. Cook until tender, about 5 minutes. Remove cucumber with a slotted spoon and cover to keep warm.
- Season chops with additional salt and pepper. Cook over medium-high heat, turning often, until brown on both sides and pink inside, about 6 to 8 minutes. Remove and keep warm. Add wine and mint to pan. Cook over high heat, scraping up brown bits, about 2 minutes.
- Remove pan from heat. Add butter and stir until melted. Place cucumbers over chops and cover with sauce.

# *Lamb Curry with Condiments*

*Unique in its flavor*

- 2 *pounds lamb, cut into 1-inch cubes*
- 6 *tablespoons vegetable oil*
- 2 *medium onions, coarsely chopped*
- 1 *tablespoon grated fresh ginger root*
- 2 *tablespoons curry powder (or more to taste)*
- 2½ *cups beef stock*
- 2 *tablespoons flour*
- 4 *tablespoons water*
- 4-5 *cups cooked rice*

## *Condiments*

*mango or peach chutney*
*shredded coconut*
*chopped unsalted peanuts*
*raisins*
*crumbled bacon*
*sliced bananas*
*chopped tomatoes, onion, or green apples*

*Serves 6*

- Heat oil in a large sauté pan over medium heat, and brown lamb cubes. Add onions and ginger. Sauté onions until soft and translucent. Add curry powder; stir to combine. Add beef stock and let curry come to a slow boil.
- Lower heat and simmer, covered, until meat is tender, about 35 minutes. With a slotted spoon, remove lamb to a bowl. Cover to keep warm.
- Combine flour and water and add to pan. Bring pan juices to a slow boil and stir until sauce is thickened, about 8 to 10 minutes. Reduce heat to low. Return lamb to pan and cook until heated through.
- Spread warm rice over a large platter and top with lamb curry. Surround platter with small bowls of condiments.

## *Swedish Mustard*

*This delicious gift from your kitchen spices up any holiday ham.*

- 4 *ounces Colman's dry mustard*
- 2 *cups bread crumbs*
- 1½ *cups tarragon vinegar*
- 1½ *cups sugar*
- ½ *tablespoon salt*
- *heavy cream*

• Beat first five ingredients together with an electric mixer. Add a small amount of heavy cream to thin, if necessary. Let stand overnight before serving.

*This mustard improves with age and will keep almost indefinitely if stored in a glass jar.*

## *Jezebel Sauce*

*Jazzy!*

- 18 *ounces pineapple preserves*
- 18 *ounces apple jelly*
- 1¼ *ounces dry mustard*
- 5 *ounces prepared horseradish*
- 1 *tablespoon cracked peppercorns*

• Combine all ingredients. Stir well. Pour sauce into air- tight containers.

*Serve sauce over cream cheese with crackers as an appetizer, or with beef or pork.*

# FISH & SEAFOOD

## *Fish*



## *Shellfish*

# *Fillet of Salmon with Mustard Sauce*

*An epicurean delight*

- 2 *pounds salmon fillets*
- 1/4 *cup butter, melted*
- *juice of 1 lemon*
- 4 *shallots, finely chopped*
- 1/2 *cup white wine*
- 2/3 *cup heavy cream*
- 1 1/2 *teaspoons Dijon mustard*
- 1 1/2 *teaspoons seasoned salt*
- 1 *teaspoon pepper*

*Serves 4*

- Arrange salmon in a single layer in a large baking dish. Drizzle butter and lemon juice over fish. Place baking dish in a 400° oven and cook, uncovered, for 15 minutes.
- In a small pan, simmer shallots and wine together over low heat until wine has evaporated and shallots are tender, about 8 minutes. Stir in cream, mustard, salt, and pepper. Pour sauce over fish. Return fish to oven; cook 5 minutes, or until fish is glazed, but not browned.

# *Sugar Grilled Salmon*

*Even non-seafood lovers will enjoy this barbecued salmon.*

- 4 *salmon steaks*
- 1/2 *cup firmly packed brown sugar*
- 2 *tablespoons soy sauce*
- 2 *tablespoons dry sherry*
- 1/4 *cup butter, melted*

*Serves 4*

- Combine all ingredients except salmon; stir until sugar dissolves. Pour over salmon and marinate 15 minutes. Place salmon over hot coals or preheated gas or electric grill. Cook until salmon begins to flake, brushing with sugar sauce while cooking. Steaks should be turned after 5 minutes.

## *Broiled Swordfish*

*Perfect on a warm summer night*

- 2 *pounds swordfish steaks*
- 3/4 *cup mayonnaise*
- 1/4 *cup Dijon mustard*
- 2 *tablespoons dry white wine*
- 1 *tablespoon lemon juice*
- 1 *shallot, finely chopped*
- 1/4 *teaspoon thyme*
- 1/4 *teaspoon garlic salt or 1 clove garlic, minced*
- *pepper to taste*

- Rinse and pat swordfish steaks dry. Combine remaining ingredients and spread on both sides of fish. Grill outside or in oven broiler, turning once, until fish is firm, about 15 to 20 minutes.

*Serves 4*

## *Avocado Swordfish*

*Tommy Smothers shared this "secret" swordfish recipe... and left us with the enjoyable task of determining proper ingredient measurements!*

- 1½-2 *pounds fresh swordfish steaks, each 1 to 1½-inches thick*
- 1 *avocado, chopped into small chunks*
- 1 *small red onion, minced*
- 1/4 *cup chopped cilantro*
- *juice of one lemon*
- 2 *cloves garlic, minced*

### *Marinade*

- 1/4 *cup soy or teriyaki sauce*
- *dash of Worcestershire sauce*
- 1/4 *cup lemon juice*
- 1 *clove garlic, minced*

- Carefully cut a large pocket in center of each swordfish steak with a sharp knife.
- Mix avocado, onion, cilantro, lemon juice, and garlic in a bowl. Stuff mixture into swordfish, securing end with toothpicks if necessary.
- Combine marinade ingredients, pour over fish, and place in refrigerator for a few hours.
- Grill over hot coals, 4 to 6 minutes on each side, until done.

*Serves 4*

# *Tuna with Spinach and Coconut Sauce*

*Introduce your guests to the sensational taste of fresh tuna.*

*1¼ cups bottled clam juice*
*5 tablespoons unsalted butter*
*3 scallions (green part only), finely chopped*
*1 small carrot, julienned*
*1 celery stalk, julienned*
*1 teaspoon peeled and minced fresh ginger root*
*1 teaspoon minced garlic*
*¼ cup unsweetened coconut milk*
*¼ cup heavy cream*
*salt and pepper to taste*
*1 small bunch fresh spinach, stems trimmed*
*2 (6 ounce) tuna steaks, 1-inch thick*

*Serves 2*

- Boil clam juice in a heavy, small skillet until reduced to ⅓ cup (about 10 minutes). Melt 2 tablespoons butter in a heavy, large skillet over medium heat. Add scallions, carrot, celery, ginger, and garlic. Sauté 1 minute. Reduce heat to medium. Add reduced clam juice, coconut milk, and cream. Season to taste with salt and pepper. Cook until vegetables are crisp-tender and sauce thickens, stirring occasionally, about 5 minutes.

- Meanwhile, melt 1 tablespoon butter in a heavy, large skillet over medium heat. Add spinach and stir until wilted. Divide spinach between plates. Tent with foil to keep warm. Melt remaining 2 tablespoons butter in same skillet over medium-high heat. Add tuna and cook to desired doneness, about 3 minutes per side for medium. Place tuna atop spinach. Spoon sauce over fish and serve.

# *Blackened Redfish*

*First Lady Barbara Bush says this always tastes best at the summer White House in Kennebunkport.*

- *3 pounds redfish, filleted*
- *melted butter for coating*
- *1 tablespoon paprika*
- *2½ teaspoons salt*
- *1 teaspoon onion powder*
- *1 teaspoon cayenne pepper*
- *1 teaspoon garlic powder*
- *¾ teaspoon white pepper*
- *¾ teaspoon black pepper*
- *½ teaspoon thyme*
- *½ teaspoon oregano*

*Serves 6 to 8*

- Combine dry seasonings in a shallow bowl; mix well.
- Dip fish first in melted butter, then in seasonings.
- Cook in a cast iron skillet, preheated until pan is very hot. Cook 2 minutes on one side, turn, and cook for another minute.

*This dish is very smoky during preparation; it cooks well outside on a grill or campstove.*

# *Orange Roughy à l'Orange*

*Folks from "Down Under" have been enjoying this fish for years.*

- *2 pounds orange roughy (or any other white fish)*
- *½ cup finely chopped onion*
- *2 cloves garlic, minced*
- *2 tablespoons vegetable oil*
- *2 tablespoons chopped fresh parsley or cilantro*
- *salt and pepper*
- *½ cup orange juice*
- *1 tablespoon lemon juice*
- *paprika*

*Serves 4*

- Arrange fish in a lightly-buttered baking dish. In a small pan, sauté onion and garlic in oil until tender. Add parsley or cilantro, salt, and pepper. Spread over fish. Combine orange juice and lemon juice. Pour over fish. Sprinkle with paprika and bake at 400° for 20 to 25 minutes, or until fish flakes.

## *Macadamian Flounder*

*How can you resist?*

*1 egg*
*2 tablespoons water*
*salt and white pepper to taste*
*1¾ pounds flounder*
*8 ounces macadamia nuts, ground*
*2 tablespoons vegetable oil*
*2-3 tablespoons butter*
*juice of 1 lemon*
*chopped fresh parsley for garnish*

- Lightly whip egg with water, salt, and pepper in a shallow bowl. Coat flounder with egg mixture. Dredge in ground nuts, coating both sides of fish.
- Sauté fish in oil and butter on medium-high heat for 1 to 2 minutes on each side, or until golden brown. Add lemon juice and chopped parsley and cook lightly. Drizzle sauce over fish and serve.

*Serves 4*

## *Crab Stuffed Fillet of Sole*

*A delicious combination that's so simple yet so good*

*8 small fillets of sole*
*salt and pepper to taste*
*1 cup crab meat*
*1 egg yolk*
*1 tablespoon chopped parsley*
*1½ tablespoons fresh breadcrumbs*
*4 tablespoons butter, melted*
*2 tablespoons finely chopped shallots*
*½ cup dry white wine*
*¼ cup Parmesan cheese*

- Place 4 fillets in buttered baking dish. Sprinkle with salt and pepper.
- Combine crab, egg yolk, parsley and bread crumbs in a bowl. Place equal portions of filling in center of fillets, leaving a small margin around edges.
- Sprinkle remaining fillets with salt and pepper and place on top of filling. Sprinkle shallots around fish. Brush fillets with melted butter and pour wine around edges. Sprinkle with Parmesan cheese.
- Bake at 350° for 20 to 30 minutes or until fish flakes easily.

# *Crispy Seasoned Flounder*

*A real old-fashioned fish fry, updated*

- *1 egg*
- *¼ cup milk*
- *1 cup flour*
- *2 pounds flounder fillets, cleaned and patted dry*
- *vegetable oil for frying*

## *Seasoning Mix*

- *1 tablespoon salt*
- *1 teaspoon onion powder*
- *1 teaspoon paprika*
- *pinch cayenne pepper*
- *½ teaspoon garlic powder*
- *¼ teaspoon pepper*
- *¼ teaspoon dry mustard*
- *½ teaspoon oregano*
- *½ teaspoon thyme*

## *Tartar Sauce*

- *½ cup mayonnaise*
- *1½ teaspoons lemon juice*
- *½ teaspoon basil*
- *dash bottled hot pepper sauce*

*Serves 4*

- Combine tartar sauce ingredients until well blended; set aside.
- Combine egg and milk in a large bowl.
- Combine seasoning mix in a small bowl. Reserve 1½ teaspoons seasoning mix; rub remainder into fish. Add reserved seasoning mix to flour.
- Dip each fillet in egg. Dredge in flour mixture. Fry in pan until nicely browned on both sides. Drain on paper towels. Serve warm with prepared tartar sauce.

## *Sherried Sole*

*Great when you're feeling rushed*

- *1½-2 pounds fillet of sole*
- *salt and pepper*
- *4 tablespoons bread crumbs*
- *3 tablespoons butter*
- *4 tablespoons grated Parmesan cheese*
- *pinch nutmeg*
- *2 tablespoons milk*
- *2 tablespoons sherry*
- *½ cup chicken broth*

*Serves 4*

- Lay fillets evenly across a flat baking dish, overlapping slightly. Sprinkle with salt, pepper, and bread crumbs. Dot with butter. Sprinkle with nutmeg and cover with Parmesan cheese.
- Combine milk, sherry, and chicken broth. Pour around edge of dish. Bake at 350° for 20 minutes.

## *Merry Ole Sole*

*Keep extra copies of this recipe on hand. Dinner guests always ask for one.*

- *8 small fillets of sole*
- *12 scallops*
- *12 medium shrimp*
- *1 cup shredded Monterey Jack cheese*
- *1½ cups prepared hollandaise sauce*

*Serves 4 to 6*

- In a buttered baking dish, layer sole , shrimp, scallops, and cheese. Cover with hollandaise. Bake at 450° for 30 minutes, or until fish flakes. Garnish with paprika and parsley.

*For an elegant touch, cut a fish shape out of puff pastry; place on top during the last few minutes of baking.*

# *Sole and Salmon Pinwheels*

*Create a beautiful presentation with this flavorful combination.*

- *4 sole fillets, halved lengthwise*
- *1 salmon fillet, cut lengthwise into 4 strips*
- *1 tablespoon fresh lemon juice*
- *zest from 1 lemon*
- *1/4 cup butter, softened*
- *1 tablespoon chopped fresh parsley*
- *salt and pepper*
- *2 scallions, chopped*

*Serves 4*

- Prepare herb butter by combining lemon juice and zest with softened butter, parsley, salt, pepper, and scallions. Set aside.
- Place smaller strip of each sole fillet on a salmon strip; roll sole and salmon together to make 4 pinwheels. Wrap one of the remaining pieces of sole around each pinwheel and secure with a toothpick. Place pinwheels in a greased baking dish; top with half the herb butter. Place remaining herb butter in a baking dish. Bake at 400° for 20 minutes, or until fish flakes easily when tested with a fork.

# *Scallops in Cream Sauce*

*Try our version of a grand French classic.*

- *½ cup white wine*
- *½ teaspoon lemon juice*
- *1 pound scallops*
- *1½ tablespoons butter*
- *2 tablespoons flour*
- *¾ cup heavy cream*
- *¼ teaspoon pepper*
- *⅛ teaspoon cayenne pepper*
- *½ pound fresh mushrooms, sliced and sautéed*
- *¼ cup shredded Gruyère cheese*

*Serves 4*

- Heat wine and lemon juice over medium heat to boiling. Reduce heat; add scallops. Simmer gently 6 to 8 minutes, or until scallops are firm. Remove from heat and set aside to cool. Strain liquid into a bowl.

- Melt butter in a pan over low heat and stir in flour. Gradually add liquid, stirring constantly. Cook sauce 3 to 4 minutes. Stir in cream, black and cayenne pepper. Cook for 2 minutes more; fold in scallops and sautéed mushrooms. Heat through.

- Spoon into scallop shells or ramekins. Sprinkle with cheese. Brown under broiler 4 to 5 minutes.

# *Scallops Gourmet*

*A wonderful addition to your next buffet*

- *2 pounds scallops*
- *1 teaspoon salt*
- *3-4 tablespoons lemon juice*
- *1 medium onion, sliced*
- *2 sprigs parsley*
- *1 bay leaf*
- *6 tablespoons butter*
- *½ pound fresh mushrooms, sliced lengthwise*
- *3 tomatoes, peeled and diced*
- *2 tablespoons flour*
- *¼ teaspoon garlic powder*
- *8 patty shells, heated*

*Serves 8*

- Put scallops into a saucepan and pour boiling water over them. Stir in salt, lemon juice, onion, parsley, and bay leaf. Cook, covered, over low heat 5 minutes. Drain, reserving 1 cup of stock. If scallops are large, cut into smaller pieces. Set aside.
- Heat ¼ cup butter in a skillet. Add mushrooms and cook until delicately browned and tender, stirring occasionally. Remove from skillet with a slotted spoon; set aside. Add diced tomatoes to skillet and cook 5 minutes; set aside.
- Heat 2 tablespoons butter in a saucepan. Blend in flour; heat until bubbly. Add reserved stock gradually, stirring constantly. Continue to stir and bring rapidly to a boil. Cook 1 to 2 minutes.
- Add scallops, mushrooms, tomatoes, and garlic powder to sauce; heat thoroughly.
- To serve, spoon scallop mixture into patty shells. Garnish with carrot curls.

# *Scallops Almondine*

*You'll go nuts for this.*

- *2 pounds sea scallops*
- *1/3 cup flour*
- *1/3 cup dry bread crumbs*
- *1 teaspoon seasoned salt*
- *2 tablespoons vegetable oil*
- *6 tablespoons clarified butter*
- *1/2 cup slivered almonds*
- *1/2 cup dry white wine or vermouth*
- *3 tablespoons fresh lemon juice*
- *2 tablespoons finely chopped fresh parsley*
- *lemon wedges*

*Serves 4 to 6*

- Rinse, drain, and pat scallops dry. If large, cut into smaller pieces. In a small bowl, combine flour, bread crumbs, and seasoned salt. Coat scallops with mix.
- Heat oil and 3 tablespoons butter over medium-high heat in a heavy 10 to 12-inch skillet until butter stops foaming. Add scallops and sauté until golden brown and tender, 5 to 10 minutes. Stir to brown evenly. Remove scallops to a heated platter; keep warm.
- Add remaining butter and almonds to skillet. Cook over medium heat, stirring constantly, until almonds are golden, being careful not to burn almonds or bits in pan. Add nuts to scallops. Add wine to skillet and continue cooking, loosening browned bits from bottom of pan. Stir in lemon juice and pour sauce over scallops and nuts. Sprinkle with parsley and garnish with lemon wedges. Serve immediately.

## *Baked Shrimp Scampi*

*Everybody's favorite*

- *1 pound shrimp, peeled and deveined*
- *½ cup butter*
- *3 cloves garlic, minced*
- *2 tablespoons finely chopped fresh parsley*
- *1 tablespoon lemon juice*
- *½ teaspoon crushed red pepper flakes*
- *1 teaspoon Worcestershire sauce*
- *½ teaspoon oregano*
- *¼ teaspoon seasoned salt*
- *½ cup bread or cracker crumbs*

*Serves 2 to 4*

- Arrange shrimp in a single layer in a shallow baking dish.
- In a small saucepan, combine all remaining ingredients except bread or cracker crumbs. Heat until butter has melted, stirring to mix seasonings. Pour evenly over shrimp, reserving 2 tablespoons.
- Add reserved seasoned butter to bread or cracker crumbs; mix well. Sprinkle crumbs over shrimp. Bake at 450° for 8 to 10 minutes, or until browned.

*This makes a great appetizer. It is so fast and easy.*

## *Country Dijon Shrimp Sauté*

*This medley of flavors creates a delicately seasoned shrimp dish.*

- *2 tablespoons butter*
- *2 cloves garlic, crushed*
- *1 pound fresh large shrimp, peeled, deveined, and split lengthwise*
- *1 tablespoon lemon juice*
- *½ teaspoon tarragon*
- *3 tablespoons Dijon mustard*
- *2 tablespoons minced fresh parsley*
- *salt and pepper to taste*
- *hot cooked rice*

*Serves 2 to 4*

- In a large skillet, melt butter. Add garlic and shrimp. Cook over high heat, stirring constantly, 1 to 2 minutes, or until shrimp curl. Remove from heat. Toss in lemon juice, tarragon, mustard, and parsley. Serve immediately over rice.

## *Hot and Spicy Shrimp*

*Wow!*

- *1½ cups butter*
- *2 tablespoons Dijon mustard*
- *1½ teaspoons chili powder*
- *¼ teaspoon basil*
- *¼ teaspoon thyme*
- *2 teaspoons pepper*
- *½ teaspoon oregano*
- *2 cloves garlic, crushed*
- *2 tablespoons chopped onion*
- *1 tablespoon crab boil*
- *½ teaspoon bottled hot pepper sauce, or to taste*
- *1½ pounds large shrimp, peeled and deveined*

- In a saucepan, over medium heat, melt butter. Add garlic and sauté until translucent. Reduce heat. Add remaining ingredients, except shrimp, and simmer for 5 minutes. Place shrimp in a baking dish. Pour sauce over shrimp. Bake at 375° for 20 minutes.

*Serves 4*

## *Shrimp and Asparagus Stir-Fry*

*A celebration of spring*

- *1½ pounds shrimp, peeled and deveined*
- *1 pound fresh asparagus*
- *3 tablespoons olive oil*
- *3 tablespoons butter*
- *3 cloves garlic, minced*
- *½ cup chopped onion*
- *1 half-ripe tomato, diced*
- *½ cup chopped flat parsley*
- *1 teaspoon chopped fresh mint (or ½ teaspoon dried)*
- *juice of ½ lemon*
- *salt and pepper to taste*

- Cut asparagus into 1-inch pieces, splitting the thick stalks and discarding all tough ends.
- Heat oil, butter, and garlic in a large skillet. Add asparagus, onion, tomato, and parsley. Cook over high heat until onion is tender, mixing often. Add shrimp, mint, lemon juice, salt, and pepper. Toss, and cook shrimp about 5 minutes. Do not overcook.

*Serves 4 to 6*

# *Shrimp Curry*

*Your guests are sure to enjoy experimenting with the many different accompaniments.*

- *3 pounds unpeeled, large, fresh shrimp*
- *1/4 cup butter, melted*
- *1 large onion, finely chopped*
- *1/2 cup finely chopped apple*
- *1/2 cup finely chopped celery*
- *1 cup water*
- *2 cups heavy cream*
- *2 tablespoons curry powder*
- *1/2 teaspoon salt*
- *1/8 teaspoon pepper*
- *hot cooked rice*

*Serves 8 to 10*

- Cook shrimp in boiling water for 3 to 5 minutes. Drain well, rinse in cold water. Peel and devein shrimp.
- Sauté onion, apple, and celery in butter for 5 minutes. Add water; cook, uncovered, over low heat for 30 minutes. Stir in cream, curry, salt, and pepper. Simmer uncovered 10 minutes. Add shrimp. Simmer until thoroughly heated. Serve over rice.

*Serve curry with several of the following condiments: shredded coconut, toasted almonds, fig preserves, chutney, crumbled bacon, sliced bananas, raisins, and chopped, hard-boiled egg.*

# *Shrimp with Apples and Snow Peas*

*As appealing to the eye as it is to the palate*

- ¾ *pound snow peas, trimmed and stringed*
- 6 *tablespoons butter*
- 4 *teaspoons sugar*
- 2 *large Granny Smith apples, peeled and cut into thick slices*
- ½ *cup finely minced onion*
- 1 *clove garlic, minced*
- 2 *pounds large shrimp, peeled and deveined*
- ¾ *cup dry white wine or sherry*
- ⅔ *cup Dijon mustard*
- ¾ *cup heavy cream*

*Serves 6*

- Microwave snow peas on high in a small amount of water, covered, about 3 minutes, or until tender but still crunchy. Rinse with cold water to stop cooking and preserve color. Set aside.
- Sauté apples in 2 tablespoons of butter until tender but not mushy. Sprinkle with sugar and raise heat, stirring apple slices until brown and lightly caramelized. Remove from skillet and reserve.
- Melt remaining butter in skillet and cook onion and garlic, covered, over medium heat until tender. Raise heat and add shrimp. Stir and toss until firm and pink, about 3 minutes. Do not overcook. Remove from skillet and reserve.
- Pour wine into skillet and, over high heat, reduce by two-thirds. Lower heat and stir in mustard with a wire whisk. Pour in cream and simmer for 15 minutes until sauce is slightly reduced. Add peas, apples, and shrimp. Stir together to combine.

*Serve with rice or noodles.*

# *Lobster Thermidor*

*Ring in the New Year with this elegant entrée.*

- *2 whole lobsters, cooked*
- *2 tablespoons minced onion*
- *1 clove garlic, minced*
- *2 tablespoons butter*
- *2 tablespoons flour*
- *1/4 teaspoon seasoned salt*
- *1/4 teaspoon pepper*
- *1/4 teaspoon paprika*
- *1/2 cup light cream*
- *1/2 cup chicken broth*
- *1/2 teaspoon Worcestershire sauce*
- *1 egg yolk, beaten*
- *2 tablespoons sherry*
- *3 tablespoons dry bread crumbs*
- *1 tablespoon grated Parmesan cheese*

*Serves 2*

- Carefully remove meat from lobster, reserving tail shells. Chop meat into small pieces.
- Sauté onion and garlic in butter until tender. Stir in flour, salt, pepper, and paprika. Cook over low heat until bubbly. Remove from heat and stir in cream, chicken broth, and Worcestershire sauce. Heat to boiling, stirring constantly. Boil and stir 1 minute. Stir at least half the mixture into egg yolk. Blend egg mixture into remaining hot mixture. Stir in sherry and lobster meat.
- Place lobster shells on a 9x13-inch pan. Fill with lobster mixture. Mix bread crumbs and cheese and sprinkle over mixture. Bake at 450° for 5 to 8 minutes.

VEGETABLES
&
SIDE DISHES

# VEGETABLES & SIDE DISHES



*Vegetables*



*Potatoes, Rice, and Noodles*

# *Mushroom Newburg*

*Rich and superb — great with a roast*

- 1½ *pounds whole fresh mushrooms*
- 4 *tablespoons butter*
- 3 *tablespoons chopped onion*
- 3 *tablespoons sherry*
- ¼ *teaspoon salt*
- ¼ *teaspoon nutmeg*
- ¼ *teaspoon cayenne pepper*
- *toast points*

## *Sauce*

- 2 *tablespoons butter*
- 2 *tablespoons flour*
- 2 *cups light cream, warmed*
- 2 *egg yolks*
- 2 *tablespoons water*

• Melt 4 tablespoons butter in a large skillet until bubbly. Add mushrooms and onion; sauté until almost tender. Add sherry. Simmer 1 to 2 minutes.

• To prepare sauce, heat 2 tablespoons butter in a small skillet. Add flour to make a roux. Add warmed cream and stir with whisk until sauce thickens. Beat egg yolks with water and blend into white sauce.

• Pour sauce over mushrooms in pan; stir, mixing well. Season with salt, nutmeg, and cayenne pepper. Serve immediately, very hot, over toast points.

## *Green Bean Bunches*

*Let this unusual presentation spark your creative energies. A combination such as asparagus tied with red pasta is equally appealing.*

- 80 *fresh green beans, trimmed, cooked, and drained*
- 8 *slices partially cooked bacon*
- *brown sugar and orange juice for basting*

- Gather 8 to 10 beans together and tie with bacon. Baste bundles with sugar and orange juice. Bake at 350° until bacon is crisp.

## *Green Beans with Warm Mustard Vinaigrette*

*Easy and delightfully different*

- 2 *pounds fresh green beans, trimmed*
- 2 *shallots, minced*
- 2 *tablespoons Dijon mustard*
- 2 *tablespoons balsamic vinegar*
- ½ *cup olive oil*
- *salt and freshly ground pepper to taste*
- ¼ *cup chopped fresh dill*

- Heat a large pot of water to boiling; add green beans and cook until crisp-tender (2 to 4 minutes). Drain well.
- While beans are cooking, place shallots, mustard, vinegar, oil, salt and pepper in a small saucepan. Heat, whisking constantly, until mixture is just hot to the touch.
- Toss hot green beans with dressing to coat. Add dill; toss to combine. Serve immediately.

## Chinese Snow Peas

*When green beans just won't do*

- *1/4 cup chopped scallions*
- *1 tablespoon vegetable oil*
- *1 pound snow peas*
- *1/2 cup sliced fresh mushrooms*
- *1/4 cup chicken broth*
- *1 teaspoon cornstarch*
- *1 teaspoon cold water*
- *2 tablespoons soy sauce*
- *2 teaspoons sugar*

- Sauté scallions in oil; add snow peas and mushrooms. Stir-fry 1 minute. Stir in broth. Combine cornstarch and water; add to peas. Cook until thickened. Stir in soy sauce and sugar.

## Apples and Red Cabbage

*Best of luck the whole year through is granted to those who serve this alongside their New Year's Day pork roast.*

- *1/4 cup butter*
- *2 medium cooking apples, peeled, cored, and thinly sliced*
- *1 medium onion, diced*
- *1 medium head red cabbage, shredded*
- *1 cup water*
- *1/2 cup red wine vinegar*
- *1/3 cup sugar*
- *1 1/2 teaspoons salt*
- *1/8 teaspoon pepper*
- *1 bay leaf*

- Cook apples and onion in butter for about 10 minutes, or until tender. Add remaining ingredients; heat mixture to boiling. Reduce heat; cover and simmer 40 minutes, or until cabbage is very tender. Stir. Discard bay leaf before serving.

## *Spinach with Sesame-Soy Dressing*

*No need to prepare a salad when serving this wilted spinach side dish*

*1 pound fresh spinach, washed, stems trimmed*
*3 tablespoons sesame seeds*
*2 tablespoons sugar*
*3 tablespoons light soy sauce*
*finely chopped scallions for garnish*

- Cook spinach in boiling water until just wilted, about 30 seconds. Remove from water, rinse under cold water, drain well, and chop coarsely.
- Heat a large skillet; add sesame seeds. Cook over medium-high heat, shaking pan constantly, until seeds are brown and fragrant. Remove from heat and grind seeds finely. Add sugar and continue to grind. Stir in soy sauce.
- Toss dressing and spinach together. Garnish with scallions and serve.

## *Spinach Soufflé Filled Tomato Cups*

*Beautiful on your buffet table*

*2 (10 ounce) packages chopped spinach, cooked and drained thoroughly*
*8 ounces cream cheese, softened*
*3 tablespoons butter*
*salt and pepper*
*grated Parmesan cheese*
*bread crumbs*
*6 whole tomatoes*

- While spinach is hot, add cream cheese, butter, salt, and pepper. Stir until cheese is melted.
- Hollow out tomatoes. Put spinach mixture in tomato shells. Sprinkle with Parmesan cheese and bread crumbs. Dot with butter.
- Bake at 350° for 15 to 20 minutes, or until spinach is hot throughout and top is golden.

## *Simple Broccoli Almondine*

*Simply sensational!*

- *1 bunch broccoli*
- *1 teaspoon lemon juice*
- *½ cup butter, melted*
- *¼ cup coarsely chopped toasted almonds*

- Wash and drain broccoli. Remove leaves and ends of stalks. Steam 8 to 10 minutes; drain.
- Place on serving platter. Add lemon juice to melted butter and drizzle over broccoli. Sprinkle with almonds.

## *Sesame Sauce for Broccoli*

*Simply sesame!*

- *1 tablespoon vegetable oil*
- *1 tablespoon vinegar*
- *1 tablespoon soy sauce*
- *4 teaspoons sugar*
- *1 tablespoon toasted sesame seeds*
- *1 bunch cooked broccoli*

- Combine ingredients and heat to boiling. Serve over cooked broccoli.

*Sauce can be used on cauliflower or stir-fry vegetables as well.*

# *Vegetables Mornay*

*The perfect combination of colors for your holiday table*

- *1 medium head cauliflower*
- *1 bunch broccoli*
- *1 pint cherry tomatoes (15-20)*

## *Mornay Sauce*

- *1/4 cup butter*
- *1/4 cup flour*
- *2 cups chicken broth*
- *1/4 cup grated Swiss cheese*
- *1/4 cup grated Parmesan cheese*
- *pinch each of nutmeg, salt, and pepper*

- Steam cauliflower and broccoli flowerets in a covered pan until tender. Sauté cherry tomatoes in butter, taking care not to overcook.
- To prepare sauce, melt butter; whisk in flour. Cook for 2 minutes; do not brown. Whisk in chicken broth. Cook, stirring constantly, until thickened and smooth. Add cheeses slowly; heat until melted. Add seasonings.
- Spoon a layer of sauce across bottom of an ovenproof casserole. Place cauliflower in center; surround with broccoli and tomatoes. Pour another layer of sauce over cauliflower only; place under broiler to brown cheese. Serve with extra sauce on the side.

## *Carrots with Raspberry Vinegar*

*Surprisingly flavorful!*

*4 large carrots*
*2 tablespoons butter*
*2 tablespoons water*
*pinch of salt*
*2 teaspoons raspberry vinegar*
*1 teaspoon brown sugar*
*chopped fresh parsley for garnish*

- Peel and slice carrots. Place in a heavy saucepan with butter, water, and salt. Cover and let simmer over low heat for 15 to 20 minutes, or until tender. Add raspberry vinegar and brown sugar. Cook 1 to 2 minutes more. Garnish with parsley.

## *Carrots and Green Grapes*

*A palate-cleansing accompaniment to your favorite fish entrée*

*6 large carrots*
*1½ cups green seedless grapes*
*1 tablespoon butter*
*1 tablespoon frozen lemonade concentrate*

- Cut carrots into ½-inch slices and cook in boiling salted water, until done but quite firm. Drain. Add butter and lemonade concentrate, allowing heat from cooked carrots to melt them. Toss to coat.
- Just before serving, add grapes (whole if small, halved if large).

## *Asparagus Cheese Bake*

*Potluck fare with a flair!*

*36 asparagus spears*
*½ cup butter, melted*
*lemon juice*
*1 pound Gruyère or Swiss cheese, sliced*
*grated Parmesan cheese*

- Trim asparagus. Cook by placing spears upright in bottom of a double boiler. Add 2 inches of boiling salted water. Invert top half of double boiler and carefully set it atop bottom half. This will give you a pot with sufficient depth to steam asparagus properly. Cook 12 minutes, or until just tender. Drain.
- Alternate layers of asparagus spears, drizzled with butter and sprinkled with lemon juice, with a layer of cheese slices. Sprinkle each cheese layer with Parmesan cheese. Top with a cheese layer. Drizzle with melted butter.
- Bake at 400° for 8 to 10 minutes, or until cheese melts and bubbles.

## *Blender Hollandaise Sauce*

*Now you can turn any vegetable into a masterpiece.*

*3 egg yolks*
*⅛ teaspoon salt*
*dash cayenne pepper*
*2 teaspoons lemon juice*
*½ cup butter, melted*

- Place egg yolks, salt, cayenne pepper, and lemon juice in a blender. Cover and blend on high for 5 seconds, gradually adding melted butter in a slow, steady stream. Blend about 30 seconds, or until thick.

*Serve over steamed broccoli or asparagus.*

## Corn Pudding

*An old-fashioned favorite*

- 2 *cups fresh corn, cut from cob*
- 2 *eggs, lightly beaten*
- 1 *teaspoon salt*
- 1/8 *teaspoon pepper*
- 2 *tablespoons butter, melted*
- 2 *tablespoons sugar*
- 1 1/2 *cups milk*

- Mix together all ingredients. Pour into greased pudding dish and bake at 350° for 45 to 50 minutes, or until firm.

## Flavored Butters for Corn

*A great way to spice up any summer barbecue*

### Dill Butter

- 1/2 *cup butter or margarine, softened*
- 2 *teaspoons salt*
- 1 *teaspoon dill*
- 1/4 *teaspoon pepper*

- In a small bowl, beat together all ingredients.
- Spread butter flavored topping over corn on the cob or cut corn.

### Chili Butter

- 1/2 *cup butter or margarine, softened*
- 2 *teaspoons salt*
- 1 *teaspoon chili powder*
- 1/4 *teaspoon pepper*

- In a small bowl, beat together all ingredients.
- Spread butter flavored topping over corn on the cob or cut corn.

### Chive Butter

- 1/2 *cup butter or margarine, softened*
- 2 *teaspoons salt*
- 2 *teaspoons chopped chives*
- 1/4 *teaspoon pepper*

- In a small bowl, beat together all ingredients.
- Spread butter flavored topping over corn on the cob or cut corn.

## *Asparagus with Caper Sauce*

*A sophisticated way to celebrate spring*

- *3 pounds fresh asparagus*
- *6 tablespoons butter*
- *juice of ½ lemon*
- *2 tablespoons capers, drained*
- *1 tablespoon finely chopped parsley*
- *1 teaspoon wine vinegar*
- *salt and pepper*

- Wash asparagus. Cut off tough ends. Peel stalks up to a few inches below tips to remove scales. Cook until tender, about 12 to 15 minutes.
- Meanwhile, melt butter in saucepan. Remove from heat and stir in lemon juice, capers, parsley, and vinegar. Season with salt and pepper.
- Place asparagus in serving dish. Pour caper butter over asparagus; serve immediately.

## *Herbed Broccoli*

*A light and delicious way to enjoy a favorite vegetable*

- *1 bunch broccoli*
- *2 chicken bouillon cubes*
- *1 cup boiling water*
- *¼ cup chopped onion*
- *1 teaspoon marjoram*
- *1 teaspoon basil*
- *3 tablespoons butter, melted*

- Wash broccoli, remove leaves, trim stalk ends, and cut into sections.
- Dissolve bouillon cubes in water in a large skillet. Add broccoli, onion, marjoram, and basil; cover with paper towels and cook quickly until just tender, about 10 minutes. Drain and add butter.

## *Stuffed Zucchini*

*Sliced into bite-size pieces, this can also serve as an hors d'oeuvre.*

- *6 zucchini (approximately 9 inches long)*
- *5 tablespoons cottage cheese*
- *6 ounces cheddar cheese, grated*
- *2 eggs*
- *2 tablespoons chopped fresh basil*
- *20 round buttery crackers, crumbled*

- Trim ends from zucchini. Boil zucchini for 8 minutes. Place in cold water to cool. Cut zucchini lengthwise and drain upside-down on paper towels.
- Combine cheeses, eggs, basil, and cracker crumbs. Mix thoroughly to create stuffing.
- Top zucchini halves with prepared mixture. Bake at 350° for 30 minutes.

*Zucchini can be frozen and reheated.*

## *Baked Stuffed Summer Squash*

*Hearty enough to be a meal in itself*

- *1/4 cup uncooked rice*
- *1/4 pound pork sausage, fried and drained*
- *3 small summer squash*
- *1 medium onion, chopped*
- *2 tablespoons butter, melted*
- *2 tablespoons chopped parsley*
- *salt and pepper*

### *Topping*

- *1 (6 ounce) can tomato sauce*
- *1/4 cup butter*
- *6 tablespoons cracker crumbs*

- Cook rice, drain, and combine with sausage.
- Boil squash in salted water for 10 minutes, or until tender. Cut in half and scoop out pulp, leaving shells. Place shells in buttered baking dish. Combine squash pulp with rice mixture.
- Sauté onion in butter until golden. Add onion and parsley to squash mixture; season with salt and pepper and spoon into squash shells.
- Pour tomato sauce over squash; sprinkle with buttered cracker crumbs. Bake at 375° for 30 minutes.

# *Ratatouille*

*The ultimate vegetarian creation*

- *1/4 cup olive oil*
- *4 cloves garlic, crushed*
- *1 medium onion*
- *1 small eggplant, cubed*
- *2 red bell peppers, cubed*
- *1 small zucchini, cubed*
- *1 small summer squash, cubed*
- *2 tomatoes, cubed*
- *1 bay leaf*
- *2 teaspoons salt*
- *freshy ground pepper*
- *1 teaspoon basil*
- *1 teaspoon marjoram*
- *1/2 teaspoon oregano*
- *pinch of ground rosemary*
- *3 tablespoons dry red wine*
- *1/2 cup tomato juice*
- *2 tablespoons tomato paste*
- *fresh chopped parsley for garnish*

- Heat olive oil and garlic in a large pan. Add bay leaf, onion, and salt. Sauté over medium heat until onions are almost clear. Add eggplant, wine, tomato juice, and herbs. Toss; simmer covered 10 minutes.
- Add peppers, zucchini, squash, and other ingredients. Stir. Simmer until all vegetables are tender. Sprinkle with parsley.

## *Celery Leaf Soufflé*

*Appealing... unusual... delicious...*

- ¼ *cup butter*
- 1 *medium onion, grated*
- 1 *cup bread crumbs*
- 1 *cup chicken broth*
- ¼ *cup cream*
- 1½ *cups chopped celery leaves*
- 4 *eggs, separated*
- *salt and pepper to taste*

- Beat egg whites until stiff. In a separate bowl, beat egg yolks. Set aside.
- Sauté onion in butter until golden. Add bread crumbs, chicken broth, cream, and celery leaves. Fold in egg yolks. Fold in egg whites. Season to taste.
- Pour soufflé mixture into six greased baking cups or one 10-inch round baking dish. Place filled cups in a larger pan. Fill pan ¼ full of water. Bake at 375° for 30 to 45 minutes, or until soufflé has set.

## *Vegetarian Casserole*

*Hearty enough for a meatless meal*

- ¾ *cup chopped walnuts or pecans*
- ¾ *cup chopped celery*
- 1 *medium onion, diced*
- ½ *cup grated Monterey Jack cheese*
- ¾ *cup brown bread cubes*
- 1 *(16 ounce) can stewed tomatoes*
- 2 *eggs*
- ¼ *cup butter, melted*
- *pinch of salt*

- Combine ingredients. Mix well.
- Bake at 350° for 45 minutes.

# *Acorn Squash*

*When the harvest is plentiful, enjoy experimenting with a variety of squashes.*

## *Bacon Baked*

- 6 *tablespoons butter, melted*
- 3 *slices cooked bacon, cut in halves*
- 2 *tablespoons brown sugar*
- *salt and pepper to taste*

## *Fruit Filling*

- 1 *(16 ounce) can crushed pineapple, drained*
- 1 *cup raisins*
- 6 *tablespoons butter, melted*
- 2 *tablespoons brown sugar*
- ½ *teaspoon allspice*
- ½ *teaspoon nutmeg*
- ½ *teaspoon cinnamon*

## *Fall Festival Filling*

- ¼ *cup firmly packed brown sugar*
- ¼ *cup butter, melted*
- 1 *cup chopped, unpeeled apple*
- ¼ *cup chopped toasted pecans*
- ½ *cup cranberries*

- Cut squash in half; spoon out seeds. Place halves upside-down in a shallow pan with ½ inch water. Bake at 350° for 25 minutes. Drain water. Turn squash upright. Combine filling ingredients; spoon filling into squash halves. Bake an additional 20 minutes, or until tender.

*Fillings can also be used with butternut squash. Increase baking time.*

# *Sweet Sweet Potato Casserole*

*How sweet it is...*

- 3 *cups sweet potatoes, cooked and mashed*
- 1 *cup sugar*
- 1 *tablespoon vanilla*
- ⅓ *cup milk*
- ½ *cup butter, melted*
- 2 *eggs, beaten*
- 1 *cup shredded coconut*

## *Topping*

- 1 *cup firmly packed light brown sugar*
- ⅓ *cup butter*
- ½ *cup shredded coconut*
- ½ *cup flour*
- ½ *cup chopped walnuts or almonds*

- Combine sweet potatoes, sugar, vanilla, milk, butter, eggs, and coconut. Blend well. Place in a 2-quart casserole.
- Combine topping ingredients. Sprinkle over casserole.
- Bake at 350° for 20 to 30 minutes, or until bubbly.

## *Brussels Sprouts with Pecan Sauce*

*A crunchy addition to a winter favorite*

- 1 *pint brussels sprouts, boiled and drained*
- ¼ *cup coarsely chopped pecans, browned in butter*
- 2 *tablespoons butter, melted*
- 2 *tablespoons flour*
- 1 *cup milk*

- Heat butter, flour, and milk in a skillet; cook and stir until thickened. Add to brussels sprouts and mix well. Top with chopped pecans.

## *Brussels Sprouts with Prosciutto and Leeks*

*A trio of special ingredients*

- 4 *pounds brussels sprouts, outer leaves removed, halved lengthwise*
- 10 *tablespoons unsalted butter*
- 3 *medium leeks (white and pale green parts only), cut into ¼-inch pieces*
- 6 *ounces thinly sliced prosciutto, julienned*
- *salt and pepper to taste*

- Cook brussels sprouts in a large pot of boiling salted water until just tender, about 5 minutes. Drain. Refresh under cold water and drain again. (Brussels sprouts can be prepared 1 day ahead. Wrap in kitchen towel and then plastic bag; refrigerate.)
- Melt butter over medium heat. Add leeks and sauté until softened, about 5 minutes.
- Add brussels sprouts and sauté 5 minutes. Add prosciutto and toss to combine. Season to taste.

## *Buttermilk Batter-Fried Onion Rings*

***A delectable side dish that makes a hamburger a happening***

*4-6 large Spanish onions, sliced*
*1 cup flour*
*1 cup buttermilk*
*1 teaspoon baking powder*
*1 tablespoon sugar*
*salt to taste*
*peanut oil for frying*

- Separate sliced onions into rings. Combine flour, buttermilk, baking powder, sugar, and salt. Dip onions in batter and deep fry in peanut oil.

## *Herb-Fried Green Tomato Rings*

***Firm red tomatoes are equally delicious.***

*4 large green tomatoes*
*1½ tablespoons salt*
*pinch of pepper*
*½ teaspoon basil*
*½ teaspoon oregano*
*2 cups plain corn meal*
*½ cup shortening or vegetable oil*

- Wash tomatoes and pat dry. Cut into ¼-inch slices. Combine seasonings; sprinkle over sliced tomatoes.
- Dip each slice in corn meal; lay aside on waxed paper.
- Heat oil; fry tomato slices until golden brown. Drain on paper towels. Serve hot.

## *Oven Baked Potato Wedges*

*The best of both fried and baked, these potatoes will earn raves.*

- *6 Russet potatoes*
- *1/3 cup olive oil*
- *2 cloves garlic, minced*
- *paprika*

- Cut potatoes into large wedges.
- Combine oil and garlic in a large bowl. Add potato wedges. Toss to coat.
- Arrange wedges on a flat, ovenproof platter. Sprinkle liberally with paprika.
- Bake in a 400° oven for 15 to 20 minutes, or until potatoes are crispy on the outside.

## *Baked Stuffed Potatoes*

*A wonderful "do ahead" dish suitable for both the plain and fancy meal*

- *4 large Idaho potatoes, baked*
- *1 cup sour cream*
- *1/2 cup heavy cream*
- *3 scallions, sliced, white part only*
- *salt and pepper to taste*
- *3/4 cup shredded cheddar cheese*

- Cut potatoes in half lengthwise. Scoop out pulp, reserving skins. Mash potatoes with a fork; add sour cream, heavy cream, scallions, salt, and pepper. Whip until fluffy. Fold in cheese. Stuff potato shells and bake at 350° for 30 minutes.

*Can be frozen before baking.*

*For an unusual flavor variation, substitute 1/4 cup crumbled bleu cheese for cheddar. Or, top your special potatoes with chives and crispy fried bacon.*

## *Make Ahead Potatoes*

*You'll never mash potatoes at the 11th hour again.*

- *12 large potatoes*
- *8 ounces cream cheese*
- *1 cup sour cream*
- *1/4 cup butter, melted*
- *dash of paprika*
- *1/2 teaspoon pepper*
- *3/4 teaspoon salt*

- Peel potatoes and boil in salted water until tender. Drain. Whip potatoes with cream cheese and sour cream, adding a little milk if necessary. Spread in a 9x13-inch baking dish.
- Before baking, drizzle melted butter over top; sprinkle with paprika. Bake at 350° for 1 hour, or until thoroughly heated.

*Can be made ahead, refrigerated or frozen, and baked at the last minute.*

## *Boursin Potatoes Au Gratin*

*Easy Elegance*

- *2 cups heavy cream*
- *1 (5 ounce) package Boursin cheese with herbs*
- *3 pounds red new potatoes (unpeeled), scrubbed and thinly sliced*
- *salt and pepper to taste*
- *1½ tablespoons chopped fresh parsley for garnish*

- Over medium heat, stir cream and cheese in a large saucepan until cheese melts and mixture is smooth.
- Arrange half the potato slices in a greased 9x13x2-inch baking dish in slightly overlapping rows. Season with salt and pepper. Pour half of cheese mixture over potatoes. Repeat with remaining potatoes and cheese mixture. Bake at 400° for one hour, or until top is golden brown and potatoes are tender. Garnish with parsley.

# *Potato, Shitake, and Brie Gratin*

*A gourmet delight*

- *6 large red new potatoes, scrubbed (not peeled)*
- *1 teaspoon unsalted butter*
- *½ pound shitake mushrooms, stems removed*
- *½ pound fairly firm Brie cheese, rind removed*
- *salt and pepper*
- *1 cup heavy cream*
- *1 clove garlic, minced*
- *1 teaspoon thyme*
- *3 tablespoons grated Parmesan cheese*
- *¼ cup dry bread crumbs*

- Slice potatoes ⅛-inch thick. Place in a large bowl of cold water and soak for 30 minutes, changing water twice. Drain and pat dry. Thinly slice mushroom caps. Cut Brie into small cubes.
- Butter a shallow gratin dish or 10-inch round glass baking dish. Layer a third of the potato slices in dish. Lay half the mushrooms and half the cheese evenly over the top. Liberally season with salt and pepper. Add another layer of potatoes and top with remaining mushrooms and Brie. Season with salt and pepper. Arrange remaining potato slices on top. Combine cream, garlic, and thyme; pour over potatoes, pushing down so that all liquid is absorbed. Cover baking dish tightly with foil and bake at 425° for 30 minutes.
- Combine Parmesan cheese and bread crumbs. Season mixture with salt and pepper. Remove foil from baking dish and sprinkle bread crumbs over potatoes. Replace dish on rack in bottom third of oven and continue baking 30 to 40 minutes longer, until potatoes are very tender and top and bottom are crusty and dark brown.

## *Saffron Rizzoto*

*Nouveau taste for an heirloom dish*

- *olive oil*
- 1 *medium onion, chopped*
- 3 *cups boiling chicken broth*
- *pinch of saffron*
- 1½ *cups uncooked white rice*
- *grated Romano cheese*

- Sauté onions in olive oil until transparent. Add saffron to boiling chicken broth; set aside.
- Rinse rice with cold water and add to onions and olive oil. With a wooden spoon, stir until rice glistens.
- Pour hot broth into rice, ½ cup at a time, and stir. As it thickens, add more soup until rice is cooked.
- Sprinkle with cheese. Stir and serve.

## *Cinnamon Spiced Rice*

*This deluxe rice pilaf belongs in the side dish hall of fame!*

- ½ *cup diced dates*
- ½ *cup dry white wine*
- ¼ *cup olive oil*
- ½ *cup slivered almonds*
- ½ *cup chopped onion*
- ¾ *cup uncooked long grain rice*
- ¼ *cup uncooked orzo*
- 1 *cup water*
- 1 *cup orange juice*
- 2 *chicken-flavored bouillon cubes*
- 1½ *tablespoons mint*
- 1 *teaspoon cinnamon*

- Soak dates in wine 30 minutes; pour off excess wine. Set aside.
- Heat oil in a heavy 2-quart saucepan. Add almonds; brown lightly. Remove almonds from saucepan with a slotted spoon, and set aside. Add onion to saucepan; cook until soft, stirring occasionally.
- Add rice and orzo to saucepan; cook until light brown (about 5 minutes), stirring often. Add water, juice, bouillon cubes, mint, and cinnamon. Bring to a boil; cover, reduce heat, and simmer 20 minutes, or until liquid is absorbed. Stir in dates and almonds; remove from heat. Cover; let stand 5 minutes before serving.

## *Any Weather Baked Rice*

*Willard Scott's rice recipe will send showers of compliments your way!*

- *½ cup butter*
- *2 (10 ounce) cans consommé*
- *1 large onion, diced*
- *1 cup uncooked rice*
- *1 (6 ounce) can mushrooms, drained*

• Melt butter in a frying pan. Add diced onion and cook to soften. Add consommé and rice. Stir, then pour into a buttered casserole. Bake at 350° for 1 hour. About 20 minutes before rice is done, add mushrooms. Continue cooking. Remove from oven and serve from casserole.

*This is also delicious with sautéed fresh mushrooms and chopped fresh parsley.*

## *Creamy Rice and Vegetable Mix*

*You won't have any leftovers.*

- *1 cup uncooked brown rice*
- *1 (7½ ounce) can chopped green chilies*
- *12 ounces Monterey Jack cheese, grated*
- *3 medium zucchini, sliced*
- *2 large tomatoes, thinly sliced*
- *2 cups sour cream*
- *1 teaspoon oregano*
- *1 teaspoon garlic salt*
- *¼ cup chopped green pepper*
- *¼ cup chopped scallions*
- *2 tablespoons chopped fresh parsley*

• Cook rice. In a large, buttered casserole, layer rice, chilies, half the cheese, zucchini, and tomato. Combine sour cream, oregano, garlic salt, green pepper, and scallions. Spoon over tomatoes; sprinkle with remaining cheese. Bake at 350° for 45 minutes. Sprinkle with fresh parsley.

# Wild Rice Casserole

*A wonderful change from potatoes*

- 1½ *cups uncooked brown rice*
- 2 *tablespoons butter*
- ¼ *cup chopped onion*
- ½ *pound fresh mushrooms*
- 1 *cup chopped celery*
- ¼ *cup chopped celery leaves*
- 1½ *teaspoons salt*
- *dash of pepper*
- ¼ *teaspoon marjoram*
- *pinch of sage*
- *pinch of thyme*
- ⅓ *cup chopped pecans*

- Cook brown rice according to package directions; set aside. Sauté all remaining ingredients, except pecans. When sautéed mixture is tender, stir in cooked rice. Add pecans. Simmer over low heat until heated through.

# Rice Ring

*Great with seafood*

- 4 *cups cooked rice (not instant)*
- *dash of salt*
- ¼ *cup seedless raisins*
- ½ *cup orange marmalade*
- *cherry tomatoes for garnish*

- Using a fork, fold salt, raisins and marmalade into rice.
- Firmly pack into a well-greased 1-quart mold. Set mold in a shallow pan of hot water. Bake at 350° for 20 minutes, or until heated through. Unmold and garnish with sautéed cherry tomatoes.

## *Fabulous Noodle Kugel*

*They will stand in line for this old stand-by.*

- 1 *(12 ounce) package wide noodles*
- 4 *eggs*
- ¾ *cup sugar*
- 1 *teaspoon vanilla*
- 2 *teaspoons lemon extract*
- 1 *pint sour cream*
- 1 *pound large curd cottage cheese*
- 1½ *cups milk*
- 3 *tablespoons butter*
- 2 *tablespoons sugar*
- 1 *tablespoon cinnamon*

- Cook noodles according to package directions. Drain.
- With a fork, beat eggs, sugar, vanilla, and lemon extract together in a bowl. Add sour cream, cottage cheese, and milk; mix thoroughly.
- Add noodles; stir. Pour mixture into a well greased 9x13-inch casserole.
- Dot with butter and sprinkle with a mixture of cinnamon and sugar. Bake at 350° for 1 hour and 15 minutes. Cool 10 minutes before slicing.

## *Baked Fettucine*

*All the rich taste of Alfredo — none of the last minute fuss.*

- 1 *pound fettucine, cooked and drained*
- 1 *pound mozzarella cheese, shredded*
- ½ *cup butter, melted*
- *salt and pepper*
- 2 *cups heavy cream*
- ¾ *pound Parmesan cheese, grated*
- 2 *tablespoons butter, softened*

*Serves 12*

- Place fettucine in large bowl. Add mozzarella, melted butter, salt, pepper, ¾ cup cream, and ¾ of the Parmesan cheese. Mix well.
- Pour mixture into buttered baking dish. Top with remaining cream and Parmesan cheese. Dot top with softened butter. Bake at 350° for 40 minutes.

*Can be made the day before.*

# COOKIES & BARS

# COOKIES & BARS



*Bars*



*Cookies*



*Specialties*

## *Butterscotch Cheesecake Bars*

*Better hide these!*

- *1 (12 ounce) package butterscotch morsels*
- *1/3 cup butter*
- *2 cups graham cracker crumbs*
- *1 cup chopped walnuts*
- *8 ounces cream cheese, softened*
- *1 (14 ounce) can sweetened condensed milk (not evaporated)*
- *1 teaspoon vanilla*
- *1 egg*

- Melt morsels and butter. Stir in crumbs and walnuts. Press half the mixture firmly into bottom of a greased 9x13-inch baking pan.
- In a large mixing bowl, beat cheese until fluffy. Beat in sweetened condensed milk, vanilla, and egg. Mix well.
- Pour into prepared pan. Top with remaining crumb mixture. Bake at 350° for 25 to 30 minutes, or until toothpick inserted in center comes out clean. Cool to room temperature. Chill before cutting. Refrigerate leftovers.

## *Brownies for Beginners*

*Homemade brownies when a "box" just won't do*

- *1/3 cup butter*
- *1/3 cup cocoa*
- *1 cup sugar*
- *2 eggs*
- *1/2 cup flour*
- *1/2 teaspoon baking powder*
- *1/4 teaspoon salt*
- *1 teaspoon vanilla*
- *1/2 cup chopped walnuts (optional)*

- Melt butter over low heat. Remove from heat. Stir in cocoa and sugar. Add eggs one at a time, beating after each egg. Add flour, baking powder, salt, and vanilla. Beat well. Stir in walnuts, if desired.
- Pour into a greased 8x8-inch pan. Bake at 350° for 30 to 35 minutes.

## *Ricotta Brownies*

*Unbelievably moist*

- 1 *cup butter*
- 4 *ounces unsweetened chocolate*
- 2½ *cups sugar*
- 4 *eggs*
- 1 *cup flour*
- 2 *teaspoons vanilla*
- 1 *cup ricotta cheese*
- 1 *cup chopped walnuts*

- Melt butter and chocolate in a large saucepan. With a wire whisk, beat in 2 cups sugar and 3 eggs until blended. (Set aside remaining sugar and egg.) Stir in flour and 1 teaspoon vanilla.
- In a separate bowl, combine ricotta, remaining sugar, egg, and vanilla. Beat well.
- Gently blend cheese mixture into chocolate mixture. Spread batter into a greased 9x13-inch pan. Sprinkle with chopped nuts.
- Bake at 350° for approximately 45 minutes.

## *Double Chocolate Hazelnut Brownies*

*Wonderful with a glass of milk or cup of tea*

- ½ *cup unsalted butter*
- 2 *ounces unsweetened chocolate*
- 1 *cup sugar*
- 2 *eggs*
- 1 *teaspoon vanilla*
- ¾ *cup flour*
- ½ *teaspoon baking powder*
- ½ *teaspoon salt (¼ teaspoon if using salted butter)*
- 1 *cup chopped toasted hazelnuts*
- ½ *cup chopped dark bittersweet chocolate*

- Melt butter and chocolate together in a double boiler. Allow to cool.
- Whip together sugar and eggs. Add vanilla and cooled chocolate mixture.
- In a separate bowl, sift together flour, baking powder, and salt.
- Stir dry ingredients into butter/chocolate mixture just until blended. Add hazelnuts and chopped dark chocolate.
- Place in a greased and floured 8x8-inch pan. Bake at 350° for 25 minutes, or until fudgy but not firm. Cut into pieces while slightly warm.

## *Lemon Bars*

*Smooth and satisfying*

- 1 *cup plus 2 tablespoons flour*
- ¼ *cup plus 1 tablespoon confectioner's sugar*
- ½ *cup cold unsalted butter, sliced*
- 2 *eggs*
- ¾ *cup sugar*
- ½ *teaspoon lemon zest*
- ¼ *cup fresh lemon juice*
- ¼ *teaspoon baking powder*
- *pinch of salt*

- Stir together 1 cup flour and ¼ cup confectioner's sugar. Cut in butter (dough will resemble coarse meal). Continue working dough with fingertips until it holds together; press evenly into bottom of an ungreased 8x8-inch pan. Bake at 350° for 15 minutes.
- Beat eggs until frothy. Gradually add sugar. Add lemon zest and juice. Beat at high speed for 10 minutes, or until smooth and slightly thickened. Combine baking powder and salt to remaining 2 tablespoons flour. Add to egg mixture. Pour over baked layer. Bake an additional 20 minutes. Sift remaining confectioner's sugar on top of cooled cake.

## *Specialty Squares*

*Makes up quickly — disappears even faster!*

- 1 *cup butter*
- 1 *cup sugar*
- 2 *cups cake flour (Wondra)*
- ½ *cup chopped walnuts*
- ½ *cup strawberry jam*

- Beat together butter and sugar. Add flour and mix well.
- Add nuts to half of batter. (Reserve remaining batter.) Pat into an 8x8-inch greased pan.
- Spread jam over batter in pan. Top with reserved batter. Bake at 350° for 1 hour.

## *Tea Time Tassies*

*Crunchy sweet!*

- *3 ounces cream cheese*
- *½ cup butter (do not substitute margarine)*
- *1 cup flour*

### *Filling*

- *1 cup firmly packed light brown sugar*
- *1 egg*
- *1 teaspoon vanilla*
- *1 tablespoon butter, melted*
- *dash of salt*
- *¾ cup chopped walnuts or pecans*
- *whole nuts for decoration*

*Makes 24 cookies*

- Allow cream cheese and butter to reach room temperature. Mix with flour until smooth. Chill in refrigerator at least 1 hour.
- In a small bowl, mix together all filling ingredients.
- Form chilled dough into balls the size of a walnut. Line small cupcake tins with dough. Fill each dough cup with about ½ teaspoon filling. Top with a whole nut. Bake at 350° for 25 minutes.

## *Honey Sand Balls*

*For the "non-chocolate" lover*

- *1 cup butter, softened (do not substitute margarine)*
- *½ cup sifted confectioner's sugar*
- *2 tablespoons honey*
- *2 cups flour*
- *¾ cup chopped walnuts*
- *1 teaspoon vanilla*
- *¼ teaspoon salt*
- *additional sifted confectioner's sugar for rolling*

*Makes 4 dozen cookies*

- In a large mixing bowl, beat together butter, confectioner's sugar, and honey. Add flour, nuts, vanilla, and salt. Mix thoroughly, using hands if necessary. Shape into 1-inch balls. Place 1½ inches apart on a greased cookie sheet.
- Bake at 325° for 14 to 16 minutes, or until cookies are barely tinged with brown.
- While cookies are still warm, roll them in confectioner's sugar. Cool. Roll cookies in confectioner's sugar again.

# *Pecan Butter Cookies*

*The pecans give this cookie a Southern accent.*

- 1 *cup pecan butter (1 cup pecans and 2 tablespoons vegetable oil mixed in food processor until a thick smooth paste is formed)*
- ½ *cup unsalted butter, softened*
- ½ *cup firmly packed dark brown sugar*
- ½ *cup sugar*
- 1 *egg*
- 1½ *cups sifted flour*
- 1 *teaspoon baking soda*
- ½ *teaspoon salt*
- 2 *tablespoons dark rum*
- ½ *teaspoon vanilla*
- 1 *cup coarsely chopped pecans*
- ½ *cup old-fashioned rolled oats*

*Makes 4 to 5 dozen cookies*

- Cream unsalted butter and sugars in a large mixing bowl. Beat in egg, then pecan butter. Sift flour, baking soda, and salt together. Stir into butter mixture with a wooden spoon. Stir in rum and vanilla. Add chopped pecans and oats.

- Shape dough into 1-inch balls and place 2 inches apart on a greased cookie sheet. Flatten balls with a fork dipped in warm water, making a criss-cross pattern. Bake at 350° for 10 to 12 minutes.

## *Almond Meringue Cookies*

*Mary Tyler Moore was sweet enough to send us this recipe for sugar-free cookies.*

*4 egg whites*
*8 tablespoons powdered skim milk*
*1 teaspoon vanilla*
*1 teaspoon almond extract*
*1 teaspoon liquid artificial sweetener*
*cinnamon*

*Makes 2 to 2½ dozen cookies*

- Beat egg whites until stiff peaks form. Add skim milk powder. Mix well. Add vanilla, almond extract, and sugar substitute. Stir to combine.
- Drop cookies by spoonfuls onto a cookie sheet. Bake at 275° for 45 minutes. Remove from cookie sheet and dust with cinnamon.

## *Chocolate Macaroons*

*Almost like a candy bar*

*4 ounces unsweetened chocolate*
*1 (14 ounce) package shredded coconut*
*1 (14 ounce) can sweetened condensed milk*
*2 teaspoons vanilla*
*confectioner's sugar*

*Makes 2 dozen cookies*

- Melt chocolate in a double boiler or microwave oven and allow to cool.
- Combine next 3 ingredients. Drop by spoonfuls onto a greased cookie sheet. Bake at 325° for 10 to 12 minutes. Remove from cookie sheet immediately. When cool, sprinkle with confectioner's sugar.

# *Chocolate Chip Meringues*

*A fluffy and incredibly light confection*

- 2 *egg whites*
- 1/8 *teaspoon cream of tartar*
- 1/8 *teaspoon salt*
- 1 *teaspoon vanilla*
- 3/4 *cup sugar*
- 1 *(6 ounce) package semi-sweet chocolate chips*

*Makes 2 to 2 1/2 dozen cookies*

- In a large mixing bowl, beat together egg whites, cream of tartar, salt, and vanilla until stiff peaks form.
- Slowly add sugar, one tablespoon at a time, beating well after each addition, so that egg whites remain stiff and do not become grainy.
- Fold chocolate chips into egg whites.
- Drop batter by the tablespoon onto a lined cookie sheet.(Cookie sheet may be lined with wax, parchment, or brown paper.)
- Bake at 300° for 25 to 30 minutes, or until meringues are golden. Cool completely. Store in air-tight containers.

# *Butterfly Cookies*

*This recipe will become one of your most treasured possessions!*

- *1½ cups flour*
- *½ cup cake flour*
- *¼ teaspoon salt*
- *14 tablespoons (7 ounces) butter, softened*
- *5-7 tablespoons ice water*
- *additional softened butter and sugar for rolling pastry*

*Makes 2 to 2½ dozen cookies*

- Sift together flour, cake flour, and salt. Cut in butter. Add ice water, 1 tablespoon at a time, until dough is proper consistency for rolling, neither crumbly nor sticky.
- On a floured surface, roll dough into a rectangle ¼-inch thick. Spread top two-thirds with 2 tablespoons soft butter. Fold bottom third up over the middle third, then fold top third down to cover it. Turn dough so that fold is to one side, and a small end is facing you. Roll dough again into a rectangle and repeat buttering and folding. Wrap and refrigerate for an hour or more.
- Spread a layer of sugar ⅛-inch thick on work surface. Roll dough, sprinkling liberally with sugar, into a rectangle 3⁄16-inch thick. Fold into three layers, as before. Roll out again in sugar and fold in three layers again. Wrap and refrigerate 30 minutes.
- Roll chilled dough again in sugar forming a strip 8 inches wide on its short side and ¼-inch thick. Fold long sides to meet in the center, sprinkle on more sugar, and press into dough with a rolling pin. Fold dough in two, lengthwise again, giving four layers of sugary dough. Cut crosswise into ½-inch slices. Turn slices of dough cut-side up and bend the two ends slightly outward forming a "Y" shape.

*Continued on next page*

*Butterfly Cookies, continued*

Place 3 inches apart on clean, dry baking sheets; cover and refrigerate for 30 minutes or more.

- Bake at 450° for about 6 minutes. Turn over and bake 3 to 4 minutes more, until nicely caramelized.

*These are temperamental and must be watched closely while baking.*

# Raspberry Confections

*This recipe is a holiday standard, passed down from mother to daughter with love.*

*2⅓ cups flour*
*½ cup sugar*
*¼ teaspoon salt*
*1 cup butter*
*½ cup grated almonds*
*1½ teaspoons vanilla*
*raspberry jam*
*additional sugar for rolling cookies*

*Makes 2 dozen cookies*

- Sift together first 3 ingredients. Cut in butter, almonds, and vanilla. Work dough with fingers until a ball is formed.
- Roll dough out very thin. Cut out cookies with a small (1½ inch) cutter. Place on a lightly-greased cookie sheet. Bake at 350° for 8 to 10 minutes, or until lightly browned.
- While cookies are still warm, spread with jam. Place another cookie on top, forming a "sandwich." Roll in granulated sugar.

# *World's Best Cookies*

*Unbelievably good!*

- *1 cup butter*
- *1 cup sugar*
- *1 cup firmly packed brown sugar*
- *1 egg*
- *1 teaspoon vanilla*
- *1 cup vegetable oil*
- *1 cup rolled oats*
- *1 cup crushed corn flakes*
- *½ cup shredded coconut*
- *½ cup chopped walnuts or pecans*
- *3½ cups flour*
- *1 teaspoon baking soda*
- *1 teaspoon salt*

*Makes 5 dozen cookies*

- Cream together butter and sugars until light and fluffy. Add egg and vanilla, mixing well, then salad oil, mixing well. Add oats, corn flakes, coconut, and nuts, stirring well. Add flour, baking soda, and salt. Mix well.
- Form dough into balls the size of walnuts. Place on an ungreased cookie sheet. Flatten with a fork dipped in warm water. Bake at 350° for 12 minutes. Allow to cool on cookie sheet for a few minutes before removing.

*For extra sweetness, sprinkle warm cookies with granulated sugar.*

# *Chewy Peanut Butter and Apple Cookies*

*A healthy treat for the "lunch box set"*

- ¾ *cup peanut butter*
- 3 *tablespoons margarine*
- 1 *cup firmly packed brown sugar*
- 1 *cup whole wheat flour*
- 2 *egg whites*
- 2 *tablespoons skim milk*
- ½ *teaspoon baking soda*
- ¾ *cup quick-cooking rolled oats*
- 1 *medium apple, peeled, cored and finely chopped*

*Makes 5 dozen cookies*

- In a small mixing bowl, beat peanut butter and margarine until softened. Add brown sugar, half the flour, egg whites, milk, and baking soda. Beat until well blended. Stir in remaining flour, rolled oats, and apple.

- Drop by well-rounded tablespoons onto an ungreased cookie sheet; flatten slightly.

- Bake at 350° for 12 to 14 minutes, or until golden. Remove from cookie sheet. Cool on a wire rack.

*To store, place in a moisture-proof container; freeze up to 6 months.*

# *"Name-Dropped" Cookies*

*Now the secret's out...so you can be "world-famous" for your rich cookies, too.*

- 1 *cup butter*
- 1 *cup sugar*
- 1 *cup firmly packed brown sugar*
- 2 *eggs*
- 1 *teaspoon vanilla*
- 2 *cups flour*
- 2½ *cups blended oatmeal (measure oatmeal and process in blender to a fine powder)*
- ½ *teaspoon salt*
- 1 *teaspoon baking powder*
- 1 *teaspoon baking soda*
- 1 *(12 ounce) package semi-sweet chocolate chips*
- 1 *(4 ounce) sweet chocolate candy bar, grated*
- 1½ *cups chopped walnuts or pecans*

*Makes 5 dozen cookies*

- Cream butter and both sugars. Add eggs and vanilla. Mix together with flour, oatmeal, salt, baking powder, and baking soda. Add chips, candy, and nuts.
- Roll into balls and place 2 inches apart on a cookie sheet. Bake for 6 minutes at 375°.

# *Giant Fudgies*

*A monstrously-good cookie to pair with a dish of ice cream*

- *½ cup butter, softened*
- *¾ cup sugar*
- *1 egg*
- *1 teaspoon vanilla*
- *1 cup flour*
- *½ cup cocoa*
- *½ teaspoon baking soda*
- *1½ cups chopped pecans*
- *1 (6 ounce) package semi-sweet chocolate chips*

*Makes 10 cookies*

- Beat butter, sugar, egg, vanilla, flour, cocoa, and baking soda at medium speed until well blended. Stir in pecans and chocolate chips.
- Drop dough by ¼-cupfuls onto an ungreased cookie sheet. Flatten dough into 3½-inch rounds.
- Bake at 375° for 8 to 10 minutes until dry to touch, but still soft. Cool on cookie sheet for 2 minutes. Remove to wire racks and cool completely.

# *Fruit Pizza*

*You make the crust; have your young party-goers add the toppings!*

- *1/2 cup butter*
- *3/4 cup sugar*
- *1 egg*
- *1/2 teaspoon vanilla*
- *1 tablespoon milk*
- *1 1/4 cups flour*
- *1/2 teaspoon baking powder*

## *Glaze*

- *3 tablespoons cornstarch*
- *3 tablespoons strawberry-flavored gelatin mix*
- *1 cup water*
- *1 cup sugar*

## *Cream Layer*

- *1 cup confectioner's sugar*
- *8 ounces cream cheese*

## *Toppings*

- *2 bananas, sliced*
- *1 (8 ounce) can Mandarin orange sections, drained*
- *1 (8 ounce) can crushed pineapple, drained*
- *8-10 fresh strawberries, sliced*
- *2 kiwi fruits, sliced*
- *1/2 pint blueberries*

*Makes 1 14-inch pizza*

- Cream butter and sugar. Add egg, vanilla, and milk. Beat thoroughly. Combine flour and baking powder. Add dry ingredients to butter mixture; blend well. Pat into a 14-inch pizza pan. Bake 8 to 10 minutes at 350°.
- Combine all glaze ingredients in a saucepan. Boil until thickened. Refrigerate until cool.
- Whip together confectioner's sugar and cream cheese to form a cream layer. Spread over baked, cooked cookie layer.
- Place sliced bananas atop cream layer. Cover completely with cooled glaze to prevent bananas from turning brown.
- Scatter remaining fruit over glaze, "pizza-style."

# *Chocolate Pizza*

*Every child loves pizza; imagine the look on your children's faces when you serve them this one!*

- *1 (12 ounce) package semi-sweet chocolate chips*
- *1 pound white chocolate, divided*
- *2 cups miniature marshmallows*
- *1 cup crisp rice cereal*
- *1 cup peanuts*
- *1 (16 ounce) jar red maraschino cherries, drained, cherries cut in half*
- *½ cup shredded coconut*
- *1 teaspoon vegetable oil*
- *¼ cup coated chocolate candy pieces*

- Melt chocolate chips with 14 ounces white chocolate in a large saucepan over low heat, stirring until smooth. Remove from heat.
- Stir in marshmallows, cereal, and peanuts. Pour onto a greased 12-inch pizza pan. Top with cherries; sprinkle with coconut.
- Melt remaining 2 ounces white chocolate with oil over low heat, stirring until smooth; drizzle over coconut. Sprinkle with candy pieces. Chill until firm; store at room temperature.

*For smaller pizzas, shape mixture into four 6-inch rounds or twelve 4-inch rounds on wax paper-lined cookie sheets.*

## *Kids' Cut-Outs*

*Why not let your cookie-elf help you with these?*

*1 cup butter*
*1¼ cups sugar*
*1 egg*
*1 teaspoon vanilla*
*½ cup sour cream*
*4 cups flour*
*1 teaspoon baking powder*
*½ teaspoon baking soda*
*½ teaspoon salt*

- Cream butter and sugar. Beat in egg, vanilla, and sour cream until mixture is smooth.
- Mix together flour, baking powder, baking soda, and salt. Stir into creamed mixture gradually. Dough should be stiff.
- Let dough chill 1 to 2 hours. Roll out dough on a floured surface to a thickness of ⅛ to ¼-inch. Cut into desired shapes and place on an ungreased cookie sheet. Bake at 375° for 8 to 10 minutes.

## *Snickerdoodles*

*Our schoolyard survey says these are the most popular cookie on the block.*

*2¾ cups sifted flour*
*2 teaspoons cream of tartar*
*1 teaspoon baking soda*
*½ teaspoon salt*
*1 cup butter*
*1¼ cups sugar*
*2 eggs*
*1 teaspoon vanilla*
*2 tablespoons sugar*
*1 tablespoon cinnamon*
*1 teaspoon nutmeg*

- Sift together flour, cream of tartar, baking soda, and salt.
- Cream butter and sugar until fluffy. Beat in eggs and vanilla. Stir in flour mixture.
- Combine remaining sugar, cinnamon, and nutmeg. Set aside.Roll dough, by tablespoonsful, into balls. Roll each ball in sugar mixture. Place 2 inches apart on an ungreased cookie sheet. Bake at 400° for 10 minutes, or until lightly browned. Remove to a wire rack to cool.

# *Ice Cream Cones*

*Homemade ice cream cones!*

*⅔ cup flour*
*¼ cup sugar*
*¼ cup vegetable oil*
*3 tablespoons water*
*2 egg whites*
*1 teaspoon vanilla*
*vegetable oil*

*Makes about 10*

- Stir together flour and sugar. Add ¼ cup oil, water, egg whites, and vanilla; stir until smooth.
- Brush bottom of a preheated 8-inch skillet with ½ teaspoon oil. Pour 2 tablespoons batter into skillet, spreading batter into a 5½-inch circle. Cook over low heat 3 minutes, or until light brown. With a wide spatula, lift and turn wafer; cook 1 minute more. Working quickly, roll into a cone shape; secure with a pick. Cool, pick-side down. Repeat with remaining batter. (Do not add more oil to skillet.) Remove picks when cool. Use cones immediately or store tightly covered.

*For chocolate cones, add 2 ounces melted unsweetened chocolate to batter; reduce oil to 3 tablespoons.*

# *Lollipops*

*Lollipops for a party — or just a rainy day*

- *¾ cup sugar*
- *½ cup light corn syrup*
- *¼ cup margarine*
- *1 teaspoon flavoring or extract (peppermint, cinnamon, or vanilla)*
- *liquid food colors*

*Makes 15*

- Line 2 cookie sheets with foil. Lightly grease foil or coat with vegetable cooking spray. Arrange lollipop sticks (15) or oiled metal cookie cutters (bears, bells, stars, trees, etc.) about 4 inches apart on prepared cookie sheets.
- Combine sugar, corn syrup, and margarine in a medium saucepan. Heat mixture until margarine melts. Stir in flavoring and food color. Continue heating mixture until it reaches soft crack stage or 270° to 290° as measured by a candy thermometer. (At soft crack stage, a small amount of syrup dropped into very cold water will separate into threads that are hard but not brittle.)
- For round lollipops, drop 1 tablespoon syrup over one end of each stick. Let cool completely. Peel off foil and wrap in plastic wrap.
- For shaped lollipops, pour syrup into cookie cutters. Let set until almost firm. Remove cookie cutters. Insert lollipop sticks.

*If syrup becomes too firm before it is all poured, reheat in microwave until it is liquid and bubbly again.*

# *Butter Crunch Toffee*

*Have one quickly, because these yummy treats will disappear like magic!*

- *1 cup butter*
- *1 cup sugar*
- *2 tablespoons cold water*
- *1 tablespoon light corn syrup*
- *1/3 cup semi-sweet chocolate chips*
- *1/2 cup coarsely chopped walnuts or pecans*
- *1 cup finely chopped walnuts or pecans*

*Makes 2 dozen*

- Toast chopped nuts on a cookie sheet in a low oven (5 minutes). Warm cookie sheet for candy.
- Melt butter; remove from heat. Add sugar; mix well. Return to heat and stir rapidly until mixture reaches a full rolling boil. Add water and corn syrup. Stir and cook over low heat to soft crack stage (270° to 290° on candy thermometer).
- Remove mixture from heat. Add coarsely chopped nuts. Pour onto a warmed cookie sheet and redistribute nuts. Sprinkle with chocolate chips. Allow chips to melt slightly, then spread chocolate. Sprinkle with finely chopped nuts. Refrigerate until cool.

# *French Truffles*

*The "pièce de résistance" of your holiday cookie tray*

- *8 ounces unsweetened chocolate*
- *4 ounces sweet chocolate*
- *1 tablespoon sweet liqueur (Fra Angelica, Amaretto, or Grand Marnier) or flavoring extract (rum, vanilla, or chocolate)*
- *1 (14 ounce) can sweetened condensed milk*
- *chopped walnuts, pecans, almonds, shredded coconut, and/or unsweetened cocoa*
- *small paper or foil candy cups*

*Makes 3 dozen candies*

- Melt chocolates together in a double boiler. Add liqueur or flavoring extract and condensed milk; mix until smooth and well blended.
- Cool a few minutes until mixture can be handled comfortably. Shape mixture into balls by teaspoonsful.
- Roll each truffle in chopped nuts, coconut, or cocoa and place in a candy cup. Store in an airtight container.

# CAKES & PIES

# CAKES & PIES



*Cakes*



*Soufflés*



*Pies and Tarts*

# *Sour Cream Pound Cake with Strawberries Romanov*

*Looks beautiful, tastes bellissimo!*

- *½ pound butter (do not substitute margarine)*
- *3 cups sugar*
- *6 eggs, separated*
- *1 tablespoon vanilla*
- *1 cup sour cream*
- *3 cups flour*
- *¼ teaspoon baking soda*

## *Strawberries Romanov*

- *1 quart strawberries*
- *½ cup confectioner's sugar*
- *3-4 tablespoons kirsch or orange-flavored liqueur*
- *1 cup heavy cream, chilled*
- *1 pint strawberry ice cream, softened*

- Cream butter and sugar, adding sugar gradually. Add egg yolk to mixture. Beat well. Add sour cream and vanilla. Add flour and baking soda; beat well. Beat egg whites until stiff, but not dry. Fold into mixture.

- Pour mixture into a greased and floured bundt pan. Bake at 350° for 1 hour and 15 minutes, or until golden brown.

- *Strawberries Romanov* — Cut strawberries into halves, reserving 3 whole strawberries for garnish. Sprinkle with confectioner's sugar and kirsch; stir gently. Cover and refrigerate approximately 2 hours.

- Just before serving, beat cream in a chilled bowl until soft peaks form; fold in strawberries and ice cream. Serve over pound cake and garnish with whole strawberries.

# *Strawberry Shortcake*

*A family tradition of strawberry picking leads to this delicious reward.*

- 2 *quarts strawberries, hulled*
- 1 *cup sugar, divided*
- 2 *cups flour*
- 4 *teaspoons baking powder*
- ½ *teaspoon cream of tartar*
- ½ *teaspoon salt*
- ½ *cup butter, softened*
- ⅔-¾ *cup light cream*
- *vanilla ice cream or whipped cream (optional)*

- If strawberries are large, slice them. Sprinkle with ½ cup sugar and let stand while shortcake is prepared. (Strawberries may be prepared early in the day and refrigerated.)
- In a large bowl, mix flour, baking powder, cream of tartar, salt, and remaining ½ cup sugar. Blend in butter. Make a well and add cream to form a fairly stiff dough. Pat dough into a buttered 9-inch cake pan or pie plate. Bake at 450° for 12 to 15 minutes, or until browned.
- To serve, cut shortcake into wedges; split each wedge. Place strawberries on top of bottom slice. Replace top slice and top with more strawberries. Top with whipped cream or vanilla ice cream, if desired.

# *Carrot Cake with Cream Cheese Frosting*

*You'll swear this is the best carrot cake you've ever eaten.*

*2 cups sugar*
*2 cups flour*
*2 teaspoons cinnamon*
*2 teaspoons baking soda*
*1 (7 ounce) can crushed pineapple, with juice*
*1 cup vegetable oil*
*1 teaspoon salt*
*4 eggs*
*1 (7 ounce) package shredded coconut*
*2 cups grated carrots*
*1 cup chopped walnuts*

## *Cream Cheese Frosting*

*6 ounces cream cheese, softened*
*½ cup butter, softened*
*pinch of salt*
*1 pound confectioner's sugar*
*lemon juice*

- Mix sugar, flour, cinnamon, and baking soda together. Add pineapple, oil, salt, and eggs. Mix well. Fold in coconut, carrots, and walnuts. Pour into a 9x13-inch greased pan. Bake at 350° for 35 to 45 minutes.
- To prepare frosting, beat together cream cheese, butter, and salt. Add sugar, a little bit at a time. Add small amount of lemon juice to moisten.

Frost cake in pan.

# *Apple Cake*

*A favorite with the young and the young at heart*

- *1½ cups vegetable oil*
- *1 cup sugar*
- *1¼ cups firmly packed brown sugar*
- *2 eggs*
- *3 cups flour*
- *1 teaspoon vanilla*
- *1 teaspoon baking soda*
- *1 teaspoon cinnamon*
- *½ teaspoon salt*
- *3 cups unpeeled, diced apples*
- *1 cup chopped walnuts*

- Cream together oil, sugars, and eggs. Add flour, vanilla, baking soda, cinnamon, and salt. Mix in apples and walnuts.
- Lightly grease and flour a 9x13-inch baking pan; pour mixture into pan. Bake at 325° for 1 hour.

# *Poppy Seed Cake*

*Different and delectable!*

- *½ cup poppy seeds*
- *1 cup buttermilk*
- *1 teaspoon almond extract*
- *1 cup butter*
- *2 cups sugar, divided*
- *4 eggs, separated*
- *2½ cups flour*
- *1 teaspoon baking soda*
- *1 teaspoon baking powder*
- *½ teaspoon salt*
- *1 tablespoon cinnamon*

- Soak poppy seeds in buttermilk and almond extract; set aside. Beat egg whites until stiff peaks form.
- Cream butter and 1½ cups sugar; add egg yolks and beat. Add flour, baking soda, baking powder, and salt alternately with buttermilk mixture. Fold in egg whites.
- Pour half the batter into a greased bundt pan. Combine cinnamon and ½ cup sugar; sprinkle half the cinnamon sugar mixture over batter. Add rest of batter and top with remaining cinnamon-sugar mixture. Swirl batter lightly to marble.
- Bake at 350° for 1 hour. Cool in pan 15 minutes.

*Freezes well.*

## *Toffee Cake*

*This cake is even more luscious the next day; however, no one in our family has ever been able to wait.*

- *½ cup butter*
- *2 cups flour*
- *1 cup firmly packed brown sugar*
- *½ cup sugar*
- *1 cup buttermilk*
- *1 teaspoon baking soda*
- *1 egg*
- *1 teaspoon vanilla*
- *6 chocolate-covered toffee candy bars, finely crushed*
- *¼ cup chopped pecans or almonds*

- Blend together butter, flour, and sugars. Set aside ½ cup of the mixture. To remaining mixture, add buttermilk, baking soda, egg, and vanilla; blend.
- Pour batter into a greased and floured 10x14-inch pan. Mix together reserved dry mix, chocolate-covered toffee candy bars, and nuts. Sprinkle over cake batter.
- Bake at 350° for 30 minutes.

## *Chocolate Cookie Cake*

*Perfect on a hot day when you don't want to turn on the oven*

- *28 chocolate cream-filled cookies, crushed*
- *½ cup butter, melted*
- *8 ounces cream cheese*
- *1 cup confectioner's sugar*
- *1 large container ready-made whipped topping*
- *1 box instant vanilla pudding*
- *1 box instant chocolate pudding*
- *3 cups milk*

- Combine crushed cookies and butter; pat into 9x13-inch pan. Refrigerate until cool.
- Blend cream cheese, sugar, and half of the whipped topping until smooth. Spread over cookie crust. Refrigerate until cool. Mix both boxes of pudding with milk. Beat until thickened. Spread over cream cheese in pan. Spread on remaining whipped topping as frosting.

# *Sugarplum Cake with Gumdrop Garnish*

*The definitive celebration cake*

- *6 large egg yolks*
- *1 cup milk*
- *2¼ teaspoons vanilla*
- *3 cups cake flour, sifted*
- *1½ cups sugar*
- *4 teaspoons baking powder*
- *¾ cup butter, softened*

## *Buttercream Frosting*

- *1½ cups butter, softened*
- *4½ cups confectioner's sugar, sifted*
- *½ cup milk*
- *1½ teaspoons vanilla*

## *Sugarplums*

- *large gumdrops in assorted colors*
- *sugar*

- Combine egg yolks, ¼ cup milk, and vanilla.
- Combine cake flour, sugar, and baking powder. Mix at low speed to blend. Add butter and remaining ¾ cup milk. Mix well and beat for 2 minutes. Add egg mixture by thirds, beating well after each addition.
- Grease two 9-inch round cake pans. Line with waxed or parchment paper. Grease pans again; lightly flour.
- Pour batter into prepared pans. Bake at 350° for 25 to 35 minutes. Cool on racks. Run knife around sides of pan before inverting to remove cake.
- To prepare frosting, cream butter. Gradually add sugar, beating well. Add milk and vanilla, beating until smooth.
- Sugarplums are created by rolling large gumdrops in a thick layer of sugar until they are flattened. Sprinkle additional sugar on top of gumdrops to keep them from sticking to rolling pin. Cut leaf and petal shapes from flattened gumdrops, using scissors. Pinch edges of petals together to form flowers.
- Frost well-cooled cake and decorate with sugarplums of your design.

# *Giant Killer Cake*

*Makes grown men weak*

- *1 cup butter*
- *1 cup water*
- *4 tablespoons cocoa*
- *2 cups flour*
- *2 cups sugar*
- *½ teaspoon salt*
- *2 eggs*
- *½ cup sour cream*
- *1 teaspoon baking soda*

## *Frosting*

- *½ cup butter*
- *4 tablespoons cocoa*
- *6 tablespoons milk*
- *1 pound confectioner's sugar*
- *1 teaspoon vanilla*
- *chopped walnuts*

- Bring butter, water, and cocoa to a boil. Pour into a mixing bowl and add flour, sugar, and salt; beat well. Add eggs, sour cream, and baking soda; beat. Pour into a greased 18x12-inch cookie sheet with sides.
- Bake at 325° for 25 minutes.
- To prepare frosting, bring butter, cocoa, and milk to a boil. Add sugar, vanilla, and walnuts; blend well. Cool cake. Frost with warm frosting.

## *Black Bottom Cupcakes*

*Elegant enough for a dessert buffet, equally at home in any lunch box*

- 8 *ounces cream cheese*
- 1 *egg*
- 1⅓ *cups sugar*
- 1 *cup semi-sweet chocolate chips*
- 1 *cup water*
- 1 *tablespoon vinegar*
- ½ *cup vegetable oil*
- 1 *teaspoon vanilla*
- 1½ *cups flour*
- 1 *teaspoon baking soda*
- ½ *teaspoon salt*
- ¼ *cup cocoa*
- *chopped walnuts or almonds*
- *sugar*

- Combine cream cheese, egg, ⅓ cup sugar, and chocolate chips; set aside.
- Mix together water, vinegar, oil, and vanilla; set aside. Mix together flour, baking soda, 1 cup sugar, salt, and cocoa; pour into water mixture and beat well.
- Fill greased or paper-lined cupcake tins ⅓ full of batter. Top each cupcake with one heaping teaspoon of cream cheese mixture.
- Bake at 350° for 30 to 35 minutes. Sprinkle with nuts and sugar before removing from oven.

*Makes 18 to 24 cupcakes*

## *New York Cheesecake*

*A cheesecake that makes New Yorkers proud!*

- 32 *ounces cream cheese*
- 1 *pint sour cream*
- ½ *cup butter*
- 5 *eggs*
- 2 *tablespoons cornstarch*
- 1¼ *cups sugar*
- 1¼ *teaspoons vanilla*
- 1 *teaspoon lemon juice*

- Allow cream cheese, sour cream, butter, and eggs to reach room temperature.
- Combine cream cheese, sour cream, butter, cornstarch, sugar, vanilla, and lemon juice. Beat at high speed until well blended. Beat in eggs, one at a time, until batter is smooth.
- Pour batter into a 9½-inch springform pan. Place in a larger roasting pan with warm water filling half the pan.
- Bake at 375° for 1 hour. Remove cake from pan and let stand 2 hours. Cover and refrigerate.

# *Party Pumpkin Cheesecake*

*A dessert for company that rates "oohs" and "aahs"*

- 32 *ounces cream cheese, softened*
- 1½ *cups sugar*
- 6 *eggs*
- 3 *tablespoons flour*
- 2 *teaspoons cinnamon*
- 1 *teaspoon cloves*
- 1 *teaspoon ginger*
- ½ *teaspoon nutmeg*
- 1 *cup heavy cream*
- 1 *pound canned, cooked pumpkin*
- 2 *teaspoons vanilla*

## *Crust*

- 1 *cup plus 3 tablespoons gingersnap cookie crumbs (about 24 packaged gingersnap cookies)*
- ⅓ *cup firmly packed brown sugar*
- *dash salt*
- 1 *egg, separated*
- ¼ *cup butter, cut into pieces*

## *Spiced Whipped Cream*

- 1 *cup heavy cream*
- ¼ *cup confectioner's sugar*
- ¼-½ *teaspoon pumpkin pie spice*
- ½ *teaspoon vanilla*

- *Crust* — In a food processor, combine cookies, sugar, and salt. Whirl to chop cookies. Add egg yolk and butter, pulsing to chop butter and to make a fine, crumbly dough. Press dough evenly onto sides and bottom of a 10-inch springform pan. Brush with egg white.

- *Cheesecake* — Preheat oven to 425°. Put cheese, sugar, and eggs in a large food processor bowl or large mixing bowl. Mix well. Add remaining ingredients and combine thoroughly. Pour batter into a prepared pan and bake 15 minutes. Reduce heat to 300° and bake 1½ to 1¾ hours, or until firm. Turn off oven, leaving cake in oven until cool.

- *Spiced Whipped Cream* — Whip cream with sugar and flavorings until stiff. Serve atop cheesecake slices.

*Spiced whipped cream is also wonderful on gingerbread, apple pie, and simple puddings.*

# *Fairy Cake*

*A light, heavenly, confection*

- *¼ cup butter*
- *1½ cups sugar*
- *4 eggs, separated*
- *5 tablespoons heavy cream*
- *1 cup flour*
- *2 teaspoons baking powder*
- *1 teaspoon vanilla*
- *½ teaspoon cream of tartar*
- *½ cup chopped hazelnuts*
- *1 cup heavy cream, whipped and sweetened with sugar*

- Cream butter, then cream together butter and ½ cup sugar. Beat egg yolks and add to batter. Sift together flour and baking powder. Add dry mix to batter, alternating with 5 tablespoons cream. Mix in ½ teaspoon vanilla. Spread batter into 2 greased and floured 8-inch round cake pans.
- Beat egg whites until stiff peaks form. Add remaining 1 cup sugar and beat. Beat in cream of tartar and remaining ½ teaspoon vanilla. Spread meringue on top of batter already in pans. Sprinkle nuts over the top.
- Place in a COLD oven and bake at 350° for 30 minutes. After baking, let cake stand in pans for a short time. Place one cake, meringue-side down, on a serving platter. Spread with sweetened whipped cream. Place second cake, meringue-side up, on top. Keep refrigerated.

# *Birthday Cream Cake*

*The ultimate birthday party cake*

- ½ *cup butter*
- ½ *cup shortening*
- 2 *cups sugar*
- 5 *eggs, separated*
- 1 *teaspoon baking soda*
- 1 *teaspoon vanilla*
- 1 *cup buttermilk*
- 2 *cups cake flour*
- 1 *cup shredded coconut*
- 1 *cup chopped pecans*

## *Frosting*

- 16 *ounces cream cheese*
- ½ *cup butter, softened*
- 2 *pounds confectioner's sugar*
- 1½ *teaspoons vanilla*
- 1 *cup chopped pecans*

- Cream butter and shortening. Add sugar gradually, beating well. Add egg yolks; mix thoroughly.
- Add baking soda and vanilla to buttermilk. Beat egg whites until stiff peaks form.
- Alternate adding flour and buttermilk to sugar mixture. Beat slowly. Add coconut and pecans. Mix well. Fold in beaten egg whites.
- Pour batter into 3 greased 8-inch round cake pans. Bake at 350° for 40 minutes, or until done.
- To prepare frosting, cream together cream cheese and butter. Gradually add sugar. Beat well. Add vanilla. Continue beating until frosting is creamy. Stir in pecans.
- Frost between layers of cake. Then, frost top and sides.

# *Chocolate Ring with Raspberry Cream*

*A medley of luscious flavors*

- *1 cup sugar*
- *1¼ cups semi-sweet chocolate chips*
- *½ cup boiling water*
- *4 large eggs*
- *2 tablespoons orange-flavored liqueur*
- *1 teaspoon vanilla*
- *⅛ teaspoon salt*
- *1 cup unsalted butter, softened*

## *Raspberry Cream*

- *1 cup heavy cream*
- *2 tablespoons seedless red raspberry jam*
- *2 tablespoons sugar*
- *2 teaspoons vanilla*

• Place sugar, chocolate chips, and water in a food processor and process until chocolate is smooth. Add eggs, liqueur, vanilla, and salt. Process until well blended, stopping processor several times to scrape sides. Add butter, one third at a time, processing briefly, but thoroughly, each time. Pour mixture into a well-buttered 5-cup ring mold. Place mold in a larger pan and fill pan with 2 inches of water. Bake at 350° for 40 minutes, or until firm to the touch and knife inserted in center comes out clean. Remove mold from water bath and let it cool one hour on a wire rack. Cover and refrigerate at least 3 hours.

• To prepare raspberry cream, whip cream, jam, sugar, and vanilla with an electric mixer until soft peaks form.

• To serve, run a blunt knife around edge of mold. Invert mold onto a serving dish and wipe outside of mold with a sponge dipped in hot water. Tap mold once or twice with a knife handle and remove. Fill center with raspberry cream. Garnish as desired.

*Ring may be made up to 3 days in advance. Cream is best prepared no more than 5 hours prior to serving.*

# *Gateau au Chocolat*

*A chocolate lover's dream, with an almond twist*

*2/3 cup butter*
*3/4 cup sugar*
*3 eggs, separated*
*5 ounces semi-sweet chocolate, melted*
*2/3 cup sifted flour*
*1/4 cup milk*
*3/4 cup blanched almonds, ground in blender*
*1/2 teaspoon vanilla*

## *Icing*

*5 ounces semi-sweet chocolate*
*1/4 cup butter*
*3 tablespoons milk*
*1 cup confectioner's sugar*
*1/4 teaspoon almond extract*
*sliced almonds*
*chocolate leaves*

## *Chocolate Leaves*

*24 non-poisonous leaves such as camellia or rose leaves*
*4 ounces semi-sweet chocolate*

- Cream butter; add sugar and beat until light and fluffy. Add egg yolks and blend; add chocolate and blend. On low speed, add flour and milk alternately, beginning and ending with the flour. Beat just until combined. With a wooden spoon, stir in almonds and vanilla.
- In a small bowl, beat egg whites until stiff peaks form. With a wire whisk, fold whites into batter.
- Grease and flour a 9-inch cake pan; line with waxed paper. Spread batter into pan. Bake for 25 minutes at 350°.
- To prepare icing, melt chocolate, butter, and milk over low heat. Beat in confectioner's sugar and almond extract. Ice cooled cake. Garnish with sliced almonds and chocolate leaves around upper edge of cake.
- To prepare chocolate leaves, wash and dry green leaves. Line a baking sheet with waxed paper. Melt chocolate in top of a double boiler. With a knife or small spatula, spread melted chocolate on underside of leaves. Place leaves chocolate-side up on the baking sheet. Refrigerate until firm. Separate chocolate from leaf by pulling apart gently. Discard green. (Chocolate leaves can be frozen.)

# *Chocolate Mousse Torte*

*Beautifully impressive, sinfully rich*

- *3 cups chocolate wafer crumbs*
- *½ cup plus 2 tablespoons butter, melted*
- *1 pound semi-sweet chocolate*
- *6 eggs*
- *4 cups heavy cream*
- *1 cup confectioner's sugar*

- To make crust, combine wafer crumbs and butter. Press into bottom and sides of a 10-inch springform pan. Refrigerate 30 minutes.
- Melt chocolate in top of a double boiler. Cool until lukewarm. Add 2 eggs and mix well. Separate remaining 4 eggs. Add yolks to chocolate mixture and blend well.
- Whip 2 cups cream with sugar until soft peaks form. In a separate bowl, beat egg whites until soft, but not dry.
- Stir a small amount of whipped cream and egg whites into chocolate mixture. Alternately fold in remaining whipped cream and egg whites. Pour into crust and chill at least 6 hours, or overnight.
- To prepare topping, beat remaining 2 cups cream with confectioner's sugar until stiff. Loosen springform pan and remove torte. Cover top with all but ½ cup of cream. Place reserved cream in a tube and pipe rosettes onto middle and top edge of torte.

# *Orange-Chocolate Finesse*

*Steve and Jayne Allen have perfected the art of making chocolate mousse.*

- *4 eggs, separated*
- *¾ cup plus 1 tablespoon sugar*
- *¼ cup orange liqueur*
- *6 ounces semi-sweet chocolate*
- *4 tablespoons strong coffee*
- *¾ cup unsalted butter, softened*
- *¼ cup finely chopped glazed orange peel*
- *pinch of salt*
- *1 cup heavy cream, whipped and sweetened, for garnish*

- Beat egg yolks and ¾ cup sugar together until thick and pale yellow. Beat in liqueur. Set mixing bowl in a pan of not quite simmering water and continue beating for 3 to 4 minutes, or until mixture is foamy. Remove mixing bowl to pan of cold water and beat for 3 to 4 minutes, or until mixture is cool.

- Melt chocolate with coffee in top of a double boiler. Remove from heat and slowly beat in butter. Beat chocolate mixture into egg yolks and sugar mixture. Stir in orange peel.

- Beat egg whites and salt. Sprinkle with remaining 1 tablespoon sugar and beat until stiff peaks form. Stir ¼ of egg whites into chocolate mixture and fold in remaining egg whites. Pour mousse into an 8-inch round soufflé dish. Refrigerate at least 2 hours.

## *Soufflé au Grand Marnier*

*Just grand!*

- 3 *tablespoons butter*
- 3 *tablespoons flour*
- 1 *cup milk*
- ¼ *cup sugar*
- 4 *eggs, separated*
- 3 *ounces Grand Marnier*

- Melt butter; slowly stir in flour. Add milk, a little bit at a time. Add egg yolks, stirring constantly, to make a thick cream sauce. Add sugar and cool. Add Grand Marnier.
- Beat egg whites until stiff peaks form; gently fold into milk mixture. Pour into a buttered ½-quart soufflé dish and bake at 350° for 30 to 40 minutes.

## *Fresh Peach Soufflé*

*Our thanks to Carol Burnett for sharing this inviting recipe with us*

- 1½ *cups peaches, peeled and pitted*
- ¾ *cup macaroon crumbs*
- 3 *tablespoons Amaretto di Saronno*
- ½ *cup butter*
- ½ *cup sugar*
- 4 *egg yolks*
- 5 *egg whites, stiffly beaten*

- Crush peaches; combine with macaroon crumbs soaked in Amaretto.
- Cream together butter and sugar. Add egg yolks, one at a time, beating well after each addition.
- Combine egg and macaroon mixtures, fold in egg whites. Pour mixture into a buttered and sugared soufflé dish and bake at 350° for 35 minutes, or until well puffed.

# *Cream of Tarts*

*What more can we say?*

- *1 cup graham cracker crumbs*
- *1/2 cup finely chopped pecans*
- *2 1/2 tablespoons sugar*
- *1/4 cup butter, melted*
- *8 ounces cream cheese, softened*
- *1/3 cup confectioner's sugar*
- *1 teaspoon vanilla*
- *2 tablespoons Grand Marnier*
- *1 cup heavy cream, well chilled*
- *fresh fruit (peaches, berries, etc.)*

• To form crust, combine graham cracker crumbs, pecans, sugar, and butter. Press into bottom of a 9-inch springform pan. Bake at 350° for 10 minutes. Cool completely.

• Blend cream cheese, confectioner's sugar, vanilla, and Grand Marnier until smooth. In a chilled bowl, whip cream until soft peaks form. Whisk cream cheese mixture into whipped cream. Spoon filling into crust and smooth top. Transfer tart to a serving platter. Add fruits and arrange decoratively. Keep well chilled.

# *Fresh Pear Crisp*

*There are not many desserts that we would make in the microwave, but this is one of them. The flavor is terrific, and it's so nice not to heat up the kitchen on a hot day.*

- 8 *ripe Anjou, Seckel, or Bosc pears, peeled, cored, and thinly sliced*
- ½ *cup raisins*
- ¼ *cup sugar*
- 2½ *teaspoons cinnamon, divided*
- ¼ *cup butter*
- ⅔ *cup quick oats*
- ⅓ *cup flour*
- ¾ *cup firmly packed brown sugar*
- ½ *teaspoon nutmeg*
- 1 *cup thinly sliced almonds*

- Combine pears, raisins, sugar, and 2 teaspoons cinnamon in a 9x9-inch microwave casserole. Mix well. Place butter in a 4-cup microwave bowl and heat on high 1 minute, or until melted. Add oats, flour, brown sugar, ½ teaspoon cinnamon, and nutmeg. Stir with a fork until blended and crumbly. Sprinkle over pears, making sure corners are filled, and press down. Sprinkle evenly with nuts. Cook in microwave on high for 14 to 16 minutes, or until mixture is bubbly. Let stand until just cool enough to eat. Serve warm or cold.

*May be served with vanilla ice cream.*

# *Pear and Almond Tart*

*Designed for those with sophisticated taste*

- *1 bottle champagne or dry white wine*
- *2 tablespoons fresh lemon juice*
- *zest from 1 lemon*
- *1½ cups sugar, divided*
- *1 cinnamon stick*
- *½ vanilla bean*
- *6 firm, peeled pears, stems intact*
- *½ cup unsalted butter*
- *1 egg*
- *1 cup finely ground blanched almonds*
- *3 tablespoons dark rum*
- *1 teaspoon almond extract*
- *1 tablespoon flour*
- *1 (10-inch) unbaked tart shell*

- To poach pears, combine champagne, lemon juice and zest, 1 cup sugar, cinnamon stick, and vanilla bean in a large saucepan. Bring mixture to a boil; cook for 5 minutes. Add pears; lower heat, and cook for 20 to 30 minutes. Turn pears very gently by rotating stems so they cook evenly. Remove pears, bring liquid to a boil, and reduce by half. Pour syrup over pears and refrigerate, covered, at least 6 hours, or overnight.

- To make filling, cream butter and ½ cup sugar until light and fluffy. Add egg, ground almonds, rum, almond extract, and flour. Beat until smooth. Spread thick mixture evenly in chilled tart shell; refrigerate while slicing pears.

- Remove cooled poached pears from syrup (reserve syrup); cut in half lengthwise, removing core and stem. Place each half flat-side down; cut into thin slices. Arrange slices on almond filling in concentric circles, overlapping as you go.

- Bake at 425° for 45 minutes, or until tart shell is golden brown and filling has puffed and browned.

- While tart is baking, bring syrup to a boil; reduce by half. Brush glaze lightly over cooked tart. Serve at room temperature.

# *"Crabb"-Apple Pie*

*Binghamton Mayor Juanita Crabb knows that any of New York State's luscious apples will produce a perfect pie.*

- 2 *cups sifted flour*
- 1 *teaspoon salt*
- ⅔ *cup butter*
- 4-5 *tablespoons ice water*

*Filling*

- 6 *cups thinly sliced, pared, tart cooking apples*
- 1½ *cups sugar*
- 2 *teaspoons cinnamon*
- 1 *teaspoon nutmeg*
- 4 *tablespoons flour*
- *dash of salt*
- 4 *tablespoons butter*
- 1 *teaspoon lemon juice*

- Sift flour with salt into a medium bowl. Using pastry blender or 2 knives, cut in butter until mixture is coarse. Sprinkle ice water, 1 tablespoon at a time, over pastry mixture, tossing lightly with a fork after each addition and pushing dampened portion to side of bowl; sprinkle only dry portion remaining. Shape pastry into a ball; wrap in waxed paper, and refrigerate until ready to use.
- On a lightly-floured surface, roll half the pastry into an 11-inch circle. Use to line a 9-inch pie plate; crust should hang over edge of pie plate, do not trim. Roll out remaining pastry into a 9-inch circle. Set aside to use as top crust.
- In a small bowl, combine sugar, cinnamon, nutmeg, 4 tablespoons flour, and salt, mixing well. Add to apples in a large bowl, tossing lightly to combine. Turn into a pastry-lined pie plate, mounding high in the center; dot with butter and sprinkle with lemon juice. Place top crust over fruit; crimp edges. Create steam vents.
- Bake at 425° for 40 minutes.

# *Apple Crisp Pie*

*Harvest time means apple crisp pie.*

*Crust*

- *1 cup flour*
- *1 tablespoon sugar*
- *¼ teaspoon salt*
- *6 tablespoons butter, cut into pieces*
- *2 tablespoons ice water*

*Filling*

- *4 Granny Smith apples, peeled, cored, and thinly sliced*
- *2 teaspoons sugar*
- *1 teaspoon cinnamon*

*Topping*

- *¾ cup brown sugar (do not pack)*
- *¾ cup flour*
- *1 teaspoon cinnamon*
- *½ cup rolled oats*
- *½ cup butter, chilled*
- *whipped cream (optional)*

- Combine flour, sugar, and salt. Cut butter into flour until small granules form. Add ice water and mix lightly until dough forms a ball. Wrap in plastic and refrigerate for 2 to 3 hours. Roll out pastry and fit into a 9-inch pie plate.
- Place apple slices in a bowl and toss with cinnamon and sugar. Fill pastry shell with apples, rounding up in center.
- Combine remaining dry ingredients. Cut butter into small pieces, and add to dry ingredients. Mix with fingers, forming a ball. Pinch off small pieces of topping and drop onto top of filling, covering all of the apples.
- Bake for 15 minutes in a 425° oven. Reduce heat to 350° and bake another 25 to 30 minutes, or until top is golden brown and apples are cooked. Cover pastry around rim with aluminum foil if browning too fast. Serve warm with whipped cream.

## *Peaches and Cream Pie*

*Couldn't be any easier!*

- *1 (9-inch) unbaked pie shell*
- *3-5 peaches*
- *½ pint blueberries (optional)*
- *1 cup confectioner's sugar*
- *1 tablespoon cornstarch*
- *1 cup heavy cream*

- Peel peaches, cut in half, and place in pie shell cut-side down. Add blueberries, if desired. Combine sugar and cornstarch and sprinkle over peaches. Pour heavy cream over peaches. Bake at 375° for 1 hour.

## *Any Berry Pie*

*Mother always made this pie with strawberries on Memorial Day and with red raspberries on the Fourth of July.*

- *1 (9-inch) baked pie shell*
- *4 cups unsweetened, fresh berries (strawberries, raspberries, etc.)*
- *3 tablespoons cornstarch*
- *1 cup sugar*
- *1 cup cold water*
- *2 tablespoons corn syrup*
- *2 tablespoons fruit-flavored gelatin mix (same flavor as berry)*
- *whipped cream*

- Fill pie shell with berries. Place cornstarch, sugar, water, and corn syrup in a saucepan and mix well. Stir and cook until clear and thick. Remove from heat and add gelatin mix. Pour over berries. Chill. Serve with whipped cream.

# *Magnificent Mocha Pie*

*Chocolate and coffee create a heavenly treat.*

- 1 *cup sugar*
- 1 *teaspoon baking powder*
- *dash of salt*
- 5 *egg whites*
- 1¼ *cups graham cracker crumbs*
- 6 *ounces sweet chocolate, grated*
- ⅔ *cup chopped toasted pecans*
- 2 *teaspoons vanilla*
- ½ *teaspoon water*
- 2 *teaspoons instant coffee*
- 1 *cup heavy cream*
- ¼ *cup confectioner's sugar*

- Reserve 2 tablespoons grated chocolate for topping.
- Mix sugar thoroughly with baking powder. Add salt to egg whites in a large mixing bowl. Beat with electric mixer until soft peaks start to form. Add sugar gradually, beating constantly. Continue beating a minute or two after all sugar has been added. Fold in cracker crumbs, grated chocolate, pecans, and 1 teaspoon of vanilla. Spoon into a buttered 10-inch pie plate.
- Bake at 350° for 30 to 40 minutes, or until browned. Cool thoroughly.
- Add water and remaining teaspoon of vanilla to instant coffee and stir to dissolve. Add coffee mixture and confectioner's sugar to heavy cream. Chill several hours.
- About one hour before serving, whip cream until stiff peaks form. Spread over center of pie. Sprinkle reserved chocolate over cream. Chill until ready to serve.

## *Famous Pecan Pie*

*Take our advice, dear, Abigal Van Buren's pecan pie will rate headlines in your kitchen.*

*1 (9-inch) unbaked pie shell*
*1 cup light corn syrup*
*1 cup firmly packed dark brown sugar*
*3 eggs, lightly beaten*
*1/3 cup butter, melted*
*1/3 teaspoon salt*
*1 teaspoon vanilla*
*1 cup pecan halves*

- Combine corn syrup, brown sugar, eggs, butter, salt, and vanilla; mix well. Pour filling into pie shell; sprinkle with pecan halves.
- Bake at 350° for 45 to 50 minutes, or until center is set. (Toothpick inserted will come out clean when pie is done.) If crust or pie appears to be getting too brown, cover with foil for remaining baking time.

## *Oh! So Simple Pecan Pie*

*Cartoonist Johnny Hart, Broome County's native son, has sent us this recipe. It's as easy as A "B. C."*

*3 eggs*
*1/2 cup sugar*
*3/4 cup light corn syrup*
*2 cups pecan pieces*
*1 (9-inch) unbaked pie shell*

- Combine eggs and sugar. Add corn syrup; beat. Add pecans and pour into pie shell.
- Bake at 325° for 30 to 35 minutes.

# *Frozen Kahlúa Delight*

*Dessert and after dinner drink all in one*

### *Meringue Crust*

- 3 *egg whites, room temperature*
- ½ *teaspoon baking powder*
- ¾ *cup sugar*
- *pinch salt*
- 1 *cup chocolate wafer crumbs*
- ¾ *cup chopped pecans*
- 1 *teaspoon vanilla*

### *Filling*

- 1 *quart coffee ice cream, softened*
- 1 *cup heavy cream*
- ½ *cup confectioner's sugar*
- *chocolate curls for garnish*
- *Kahlúa, optional*

- Beat egg whites until frothy; add baking powder beating slightly. Gradually add sugar and salt, beating until thick and glossy. Fold in wafer crumbs, pecans and vanilla.
- Spoon meringue into buttered 9-inch pie pan. Using back of spoon, shape meringue up sides of pan. Bake at 350° for 30 minutes. Cool completely.
- Spread ice cream evenly over crust. Cover with aluminum foil and freeze overnight.
- Combine heavy cream and sugar; beat until light and fluffy. Spread over ice cream. Garnish with chocolate curls; freeze until firm.
- Let stand at room temperature for 10 minutes before serving. Pour 1 tablespoon of Kahlúa over each serving, if desired.

# *Fresh Lime Pie with Macadamia Crust*

*Spectacular ending to any meal*

- *1 (3½ ounce) jar roasted macadamia nuts, rinsed and dried*
- *1 cup fine vanilla wafer cookie crumbs (about 26 cookies)*
- *1 tablespoon sugar*
- *¼ cup butter, melted*

## *Filling*

- *½ cup plus 2 tablespoons fresh lime juice*
- *1 teaspoon unflavored gelatin*
- *3 egg yolks*
- *1 (14 ounce) can sweetened condensed milk*
- *1 teaspoon lime zest*
- *1 cup heavy cream, whipped*

- Place nuts on cookie sheet and toast at 350° for 2 minutes, or until golden brown, stirring several times. Remove from oven and cool completely. Grind ½ cup nuts in food processor.
- In a medium bowl, combine ground nuts, cookie crumbs, sugar, and butter. Press mixture into a 9-inch pie pan. Bake at 350° until browned, about 10 minutes. Cool.
- Place 2 tablespoons lime juice in a small bowl and sprinkle with gelatin; let stand until softened, about 10 minutes.
- Whisk egg yolks and condensed milk in a medium saucepan to blend. Whisk in ½ cup lime juice; stir over medium heat for 6 minutes to cook egg (do not boil). Add gelatin mixture and lime zest and stir until gelatin dissolves.
- Pour into prepared crust and refrigerate until set, about 6 hours or overnight.
- When ready to serve, spread whipped cream over pie. Chop remaining nuts and sprinkle over cream.

# *Mom's Frozen Lemon Pie*

*Cool and refreshing!*

- *crushed vanilla wafers*
- 3 *eggs, separated*
- ½ *cup plus 2 tablespoons sugar*
- 4 *tablespoons fresh lemon juice*
- *zest from 1 lemon*
- 1 *cup heavy cream*

- Line a 9-inch round pan with foil. Put in layer of vanilla wafer crumbs.
- Mix egg yolks, ½ cup sugar, lemon juice, and zest in a saucepan. Gently cook until thick, stirring constantly. Cool.
- Beat egg whites with remaining 2 tablespoons sugar. Whip heavy cream. Add egg whites and cream to first mixture. Pour filling into prepared pan and top with a sprinkling of more crumbs. Freeze for several hours, or overnight.

# *Frozen Peanut Butter Pie*

*Melts in your mouth!*

- 2⅓ *cups graham cracker crumbs*
- ¾ *cup butter, melted*
- ⅓ *cup sugar*
- ⅔ *cup cocoa, sifted*

## *Filling*

- 2¾ *pints vanilla ice cream*
- ½ *cup peanut butter*
- 2 *ounces semi-sweet chocolate chips*

## *Sauce*

- ½ *cup sugar*
- ⅓ *cup water*
- 1 *tablespoon corn syrup*
- 2¼ *ounces sweet chocolate, grated*
- ¼ *cup heavy cream*

- Combine graham cracker crumbs, butter, ⅓ cup sugar, and cocoa. Press firmly into a 9-inch pie plate to make a solid bottom crust. Freeze until ready to use.
- By hand, mix together ice cream, peanut butter, and chocolate chips. Spoon into crust. Freeze until solid, about 2 hours, or overnight.
- To make chocolate sauce, combine ½ cup sugar, water, corn syrup, and sweet chocolate in a saucepan. Bring to a boil. Remove from heat and stir until smooth. In a separate saucepan, bring cream to a boil. Stir into chocolate mixture until smooth.

*Serve pie drizzled with chocolate sauce and topped with whipped cream.*

# CONTRIBUTORS



The Cookbook Committee expresses its appreciation to the following League members and friends who shared their recipes and gave unselfishly of their time and talents. Each recipe has been tested for accuracy and excellence. We regret that many recipes could not be included due to similarity or availability of space. A special thanks to our families for being so patient and supportive throughout the production of *Family & Company.*

Marilyn Ahearn
Mary Beth Allen
Olive Allen
Eleanor Anderson
Liz Anderson
Diana Auchter
Tom Auchter
Cindy Barber
Karen Barnett
Jane Benas
Mrs. C. Berlinghof
Penny Besculides
Nancy Bettencourt
Eileen Birchenough
Diane Bogdan
Carol Booth
Alicia Goode Brewster
Jetta Brouker
Sue Bucci
Debbie Buglione
Sheelagh Burton
Caroline Capwell
Cindy Cerretani
Joanne Cerretani
Maryann Cerretani
Rose Claudia
Mary Jane Cleveland
Mark Coleman
Patti Collins
Trina Cooney
Joyce Cornelius
Esther Couper
Deborah Crane
Pokey Crocker
Marilyn Cruess
Bobbie Crum-Phipps
Mary Cuddeback
Mary Kay Curley
Leslie Dahlgren
Edwina D'Amore
Nene Davidge
Tish Davis
Sue Decker
Theresa DeLorenzo
Lori Dietz
Eve DiMenna
Elmer Dino
Ruth Dino
Cheryl DiPasquale
Lisa Docster
Lucille Dougherty
Jane Driscoll
Diane Dunn
Sharon Elliott
William Evans
Adele Everett
Joanne Fahrenz
Helen Fahy
Kathy Fahy
Val Farrell
Colleen Fitzsimmons
Mary Foley
Lori Freeman
Susan Fucinato
Mary Ann Gaetani
Helen Gamble
Carol Gardner
Martha Gebler
Joyce Gibbs
Sally Gieguсz
Kathy Gitto
Linda Glajch
Jane Gold
Carey Gorgrant
Debbie Gouldin
Nancy Granger
Nita Greenlee
Betty Griffiths
Sandy Griffiths
Gladys Hall
Lorraine Halwachs
Maureen Hankin
Peter Hankin
Nancy Hargrave
Mary Jo Harris
Michelle Harris
Ann Hawk
Karen Heim
Carol Henry
Sue Herzog
Carole Hillis
Nancy Howard
William Hudanich
Maria Ilioff
Betsy Johnson
Mary Keane Kacher
Jean Kaknes
Debbie Kamlet
Bonnie Kanas
Lois Karns
Shirley Keller
Jo Kelley
Martha Kerschensteiner
Ann King
Maria Kirk
Maureen Kline
Pam Kretsch
Cindy Kuhnen
Connie Kuhnen
Andy Lacey
Joan Lacey

Lynne Lacey
Rob Lacey
Dorie Lauder
Becky LaMack-Lupo
Kathy LaVelle-Tomko
Mary Ellen Leake
Fran Libous
Ann Lynch
Karen Madsen
Rosemary Mahoney
Kristy Mansfield
Mary Marrer
Sheri Masse
Karen McClure
Debbie McCoy
Janie McGovern
Judi McHale
Georgina McLaughlin
Mrs. J. P. McLaughlin
Sandy Murphy Mead
Lois Minnich
Pam Monk
Charlotte Moore
Sue Moore
Gillian Morse
Mary Murphy
Kim Stack Myers
Jill Neebe
Mary Nuckols
Libby O'Connor
Pat O'Connor-Allen
Adriane Papazian
Celeste Pazzaglini-Mack
Jill Pearis
Carole Peduto
Sue Pellicciotti
Carmen Penna
Beth Perenyi
Sue Peterson
Maggie Pevear
Debbie Pichette
Bobbie Pool
Betty Prenosil
Beth Ramsey
Marilyn Rattman
Sandy Ratvasky
Linda Rein
Carol Resseguie
Anne Reyen
Chris Reynolds
Debbie Riley
Maureen Riley
Carol Robertson
Kathy Robilotto
Rose Ehrich Romaldini
Cindy Rotella
Lana Rouff
Connie Russell
Debbie Russell
Debi Sbarra
Nancy Scala
Sally Scarpino
Janet Schuman
Alice Schwartz
Gail Sciamanna
Phil Sciamanna
Valerie Seketa
Nancy Shaefer
Ruth Shenk
Nancy Sherwood
Linda Shumaker
Nancy Shuman
Kip Shuta
Eileen Sitnik
Sue Sprout
Denise Stack
Donna Stack
Kate Stacy
Tricia Stange
Carole Stanley
Jackie Stefanski
Nancy Stefanski
Joyce Sullivan
Martin Tate
Rose Teegarden
Sue Terpak
Edwina Thomas
Mary Tomassi
Angie Traverse
Gwynne Troy
Sis Tuholski
Holly Ulmer-Strauss
Jennifer Vail
Ann Van Atta
Sue Vitanza
Nancy Walter
Michele Chuma Wasser
Karen Weinert-Kim
Lauren Weaver
Jane Williams
Roy Williams
Patty Wilson
Barbara Work
Carol Yeager
Lisa Zayac
Tia Zink

# INDEX



## A



## B

## C

# INDEX

# INDEX

## Q



## R

# INDEX

# INDEX

# INDEX

**FAMILY & Company**
Junior League of Binghamton, Inc.
55 Main Street
Binghamton, New York 13905
607-722-3326

Please send ________copies of **FAMILY & Company** @ $ 18.95 ________
Add postage and handling @ $ 2.50 ________
Add for gift wrap* @ $ 1.00 ________
TOTAL ________

Please make check payable to Junior League of Binghamton

SHIP TO: Name ________________________________

Address ________________________________

City ________________________State _____Zip ________

*If gift, enclosure card to read ________________________________

- - - - - - - - - - - - - - - - - - - - - - - - - - - - - -

**FAMILY & Company**
Junior League of Binghamton, Inc.
55 Main Street
Binghamton, New York 13905
607-722-3326

Please send ________copies of **FAMILY & Company** @ $ 18.95 ________
Add postage and handling @ $ 2.50 ________
Add for gift wrap* @ $ 1.00 ________
TOTAL ________

Please make check payable to Junior League of Binghamton

SHIP TO: Name ________________________________

Address ________________________________

City ________________________State _____Zip ________

*If gift, enclosure card to read ________________________________

I would like to see **FAMILY & Company** in the following stores in my area:

Store Name ______________________________________________

Address ________________________________________________

City ___________________________ State _______ Zip ________

Store Name ______________________________________________

Address ________________________________________________

City ___________________________ State _______ Zip ________

Store Name ______________________________________________

Address ________________________________________________

City ___________________________ State _______ Zip ________

- - - - - - - - - - - - - - - - - - - - - - - - - - - - - -

I would like to see **FAMILY & Company** in the following stores in my area:

Store Name ______________________________________________

Address ________________________________________________

City ___________________________ State _______ Zip ________

Store Name ______________________________________________

Address ________________________________________________

City ___________________________ State _______ Zip ________

Store Name ______________________________________________

Address ________________________________________________

City ___________________________ State _______ Zip ________

**FAMILY & Company**
Junior League of Binghamton, Inc.
55 Main Street
Binghamton, New York 13905
607-722-3326

Please send ________copies of **FAMILY & Company** @ $ 18.95 ________
Add postage and handling @ $ 2.50 ________
Add for gift wrap* @ $ 1.00 ________
TOTAL ________

Please make check payable to Junior League of Binghamton

SHIP TO: Name ________________________________

Address ________________________________

City ____________________ State _____ Zip _______

*If gift, enclosure card to read ________________________

- - - - - - - - - - - - - - - - - - - - - - - - -

**FAMILY & Company**
Junior League of Binghamton, Inc.
55 Main Street
Binghamton, New York 13905
607-722-3326

Please send ________copies of **FAMILY & Company** @ $ 18.95 ________
Add postage and handling @ $ 2.50 ________
Add for gift wrap* @ $ 1.00 ________
TOTAL ________

Please make check payable to Junior League of Binghamton

SHIP TO: Name ________________________________

Address ________________________________

City ____________________ State _____ Zip _______

*If gift, enclosure card to read ________________________

I would like to see **FAMILY & Company** in the following stores in my area:

Store Name ______________________________________________

Address _________________________________________________

City ____________________________ State __________ Zip __________

Store Name ______________________________________________

Address _________________________________________________

City ____________________________ State __________ Zip __________

Store Name ______________________________________________

Address _________________________________________________

City ____________________________ State __________ Zip __________

- - - - - - - - - - - - - - - - - - - - - - - - - - -

I would like to see **FAMILY & Company** in the following stores in my area:

Store Name ______________________________________________

Address _________________________________________________

City ____________________________ State __________ Zip __________

Store Name ______________________________________________

Address _________________________________________________

City ____________________________ State __________ Zip __________

Store Name ______________________________________________

Address _________________________________________________

City ____________________________ State __________ Zip __________